Pod Life

Pod Life

Podcasters' Stories

ROBERT SOUTHGATE

MARTHA W. SOUTHGATE

To book Robert Southgate and/or Martha W. Southgate for a speaking engagement, visit speakers.smgpods.com.

For more information about this book and other books by SMG Books, visit smgbooks.smgpods.com.

Edited by Martha W. Southgate, Robert Southgate, and Dani Mohrbach.

Cover design by Robert Southgate.

Southgate, Robert.
Pod Life: Podcaster's Stories / Robert Southgate and Martha W. Southgate.- 1st ed.
ISBN: 9781522043591

Imprint: Independently published

Find @PodLifeTheBook on Facebook, Twitter, and Instagram

Dedicated to the cinematic masterpiece UHF

CONTENTS

INTRODUCTION

By Rob & Martha Southgate

One of the inspirations for Pod Life was an episode of *This American Life* titled, "24 Hours at the Golden Apple." The team from *This American Life* documented a single day at this famous Chicago diner. What they captured were glimpses into the lives of regular people. It was fascinating! It was the kind of content we wanted to create.

Pod Life is an opportunity to give podcasters a place to share their journey in an entirely different way. Very often, on their shows, podcasters are busy discussing the topic and rarely talk about themselves. This is a way for us to capture their stories.

We sent out some questions and guidelines for the contributors and we were blown away by the responses. What we received back was vulncrable, inspirational, encouraging, helpful and honest. These are their stories. This is what you hold in your hands. This is Pod Life.

Pod Life

Robert Southgate

I have always loved audio. I grew up in a family that listened to talk radio and music constantly, not just in the car. I have distinct memories of, when staying over at my grandparents, waking up early and finding my grandfather was already up, sitting in his chair, listening to talk radio on a little transistor radio. I would go out and sit on the couch near him, and quietly listen along, partly because it was my grandfather and I wanted to be with him, and partly because I was drawn to the sound of radio like a moth to a flame. The problem was that talk radio rarely touched on the things I was interested in. In today's world, one easily changes the channel to find content addressing one of their passions, but back then the choices were extremely limited. Plus, radio was fairly formal, coming out of the age of announcers and traditional disc jockeys. The airwaves were filled with professionals, not the real voices I heard around me. In the media, extended conversation, stream of consciousness talk, and freethinking discussion were a real rarity. I knew what I wanted out of radio, but it was difficult to find.

When I was four I got my first cassette recorder. It was the old, blocky, rectangular type with the buttons toward the front and a speaker at the back. It didn't have a radio built-in so it wasn't a passive toy; I had to create in order to use it. I immediately took it into my bedroom and recorded myself doing a radio show. At first, I was imitating the types of shows my family listened to and played around with talking records up like a real DJ. Within the first half-hour of doing this, I already tried to break format and started talking about comics and TV from my perspective. I was trying to create the content that I would want to listen to. I could hear what I wanted in my head, and now had a way to get it out.

When I was in Jr. High, I discovered *Steve and Garry* on the radio station WLS. This was a rock station that had personalities, not just DJs. Steve Dahl and Garry Meier were a revelation to me. The other personality-driven shows were just extensions of the old-style radio I had listened to sitting with my grandfather. Those other shows were informative or discussion-based, and sometimes somewhat humorous, but *Steve and Garry* offered something different. Their show was personal and freethinking in ways no other show was. It seemed like they turned on the microphones and simply had a conversation between friends about anything and everything. The show still didn't always cater to my passions, but it was light years closer to what I craved than anything else I had found.

I had dreams of starting a radio station that would be focused on the subjects I cared about; movies,

---

comics, music, books, TV, and video games. I could hear it in my head as clearly as if I turned on the radio. Although it didn't exist yet, there were glimpses of this in reality because shows like *Art Bell Coast to Coast* and *The Doctor Demento* Show were syndicated and had become available to me. These were niche shows that were all about passion and the hosts had a genuine interest in their topics. In my early twenties, I heard about radio stations across the country, putting niche content on non-drive times. Kim "Howard" Johnson had a show about comic books on Sunday mornings on a small local Chicago station that I would get up and record so I could listen to whenever I wanted. Howard's show was followed by *The Joe Who Show*, which covered the paranormal. Both shows were about specific interests and the hosts were very passionate about the subjects. The rest of the time the station featured music. I was getting closer to my vision, but still far from it.

In my late twenties, I got a used reel-to-reel recorder. I started playing around with the idea of creating audio dramas, a practice that was pretty much dead since television took over. I had this idea to take comic books and turn them into radio plays, complete with sound effects and good voice acting, but to sell them at bookstores rather than try and get them on the radio. This evolved into wanting to take properties like *Speed Racer* or *Quantum Leap* and creating original audio dramas in the same way. The problem for this, and all my ideas around this, was the barrier to entry was much too high. I pushed these ideas aside yet did not abandon them. I knew a day would come that I would figure this all out.

The first time I heard the word podcast was an article about Kevin Smith in a film magazine. He had started a podcast with his friend, Scott Mosier, and he was as excited about the medium as he was about indie film. He half-joked that he might give up filmmaking because he loved podcasting so much. The problem was that I couldn't find where podcasts were available, much less how to listen to them. I kept thinking about what this new medium could mean and became obsessed with learning more. I quickly figured out that podcasts were on iTunes, but there were very few. I was able to download them on my iPod and listen at my leisure. The podcast medium was a giant leap forward to achieving the dream of my four-year-old self.

I became obsessed. I tried new shows all the time just to hear how people were using this exciting new format. Being a marketer at heart, I became obsessed with the business of podcasting and content marketing using podcasts. I started my career as a podcaster in February of 2013. From there, my wife Martha and I built a podcast network of over 100 shows. Podcasting has provided us with the canvas to express ideas and lean into our passions like never before. We have since performed hundreds of live podcasts, run live podcast marathons and events, and hosted panels around the country. Podcasting is my full-time job.

I love podcasts. I love the diversity of voices and ideas. I love the creativity. I love what podcasting is, what it does, and how the platform offers everyone a chance to be heard. Podcasting has changed my life in immeasurable ways. I have finally been able to fulfill the dream I had as a kid. My vision came true.

I cannot wait to see what the future brings and how far I can stretch this medium.

Robert Southgate has appeared as a host on *New Media Lab with Robert Southgate, 'Nuff Said, Live at the Blue Box, Ever After: The Once Upon a Time Podcast, Ever After in Wonderland, Coo Coo For Who: The Doctor Who Podcast, The Chester's Mill Report, Binge Worthy, This Week in Geek, Baker Street, In Hoff We Trust, The Newcastle Crew, Maybe Not the Worst Podcast Ever, Disturbed: The American Horror Story Podcast, Geektastic Cage Match, Creative Impulse, Input Junkie, The Killing Podcast, Orange is the New Black Podcast, Second Mass Report, Otherworld Theatre Presents: Gateways, Zero Hour, The Falling Skies Podcast, Tour de Cons, The Podcast Without Fear, Counter Culture, Reel Idiots, Pop Culture Countdown, Trivia Mayhem,* and *Music Under Glass.*

Aaron B. Peterson

If I could break every question I'm ever asked about podcasting down to its fundamental core, it would be "Why?" It's a question I've often pondered myself throughout this journey within the Internet. It's one my family has asked numerous times as I pass on events or outings to record another episode, and it's #1 on the list of every outsider who thinks it is some narcissistic need to hear my voice. WHY do I do this?

Many people had a difficult childhood, and I was no exception. I grew up relatively poor, and my mother was a single woman, working and putting herself through school while simultaneously trying to both raise me and keep me out of trouble. And I was a fan of trouble, defying authoritarian archetypes and finding my own path. The one semblance of peace in my mind for many of those years was when my mother and I would hit the local cinema and spend a couple of hours away from the ails of the world, engulfed in moving pictures on the big screen. This was, and still is, my happy place.

As a man, I had planned to live big dreams. I would shove off to Hollywood and embrace my dream of becoming a screenwriter. Life had other plans for me though, and I chose a more rewarding life of raising a family. But that itch remained. It never faltered.

I became consumed with entertainment media; how it was being presented as either pretentious snobbery or nothing more than celebrity gossip. I wanted, I NEEDED, more. I spent an inordinate amount of time with my IT guru friend, Rob. He helped me launch a website called *Let's Talk About Movies*. It never took off – which I'm thankful for now - but I was learning the nuts and bolts, creating the code necessary to try again. We relaunched as *The Hollywood Outsider* a few years later. The initial plan was to provide film and TV news in an outlet that felt very everyman and less "snooty film critic". This was the late '90s and *Ain't It Cool News* beat us to the punch. In the early aughts, *The Hollywood Outsider* ultimately proved unworthy of the work it took to keep up.

But itches are hard to rid yourself of unless you get them scratched.

Around 2010, my friend Scott needed my help. He was bouncing off the walls with an idea to launch a gaming podcast, Internet radio on-demand. He vaguely knew what he wanted to do, but had no idea how to do it, and I honestly had nothing better to do. I knew enough about coding and recording to be dangerous and used that as a springboard to learn the ins-and-outs of podcasting; what equipment to buy, software to use, crafting a solid format, and how to get your voice out there. If there was one thing I knew, it was how to teach myself something I had no business knowing.

As we got into Scott's endeavor, it dawned on me: this just might be my scratch.

At that time, movie and TV podcasts were pretty basic. They talked about the films they loved or loathed, or they focused on news, and that was it. Sometimes they followed one TV show, and that was it. And what many had in common was monotony to the conversation or that pretentious tone that still boils my blood to this day. You know what I'm talking about; when you're gushing about a movie that is more visual splendor than intellectual feeding frenzy and then some guy has to jump on his soapbox of jackassery with a diatribe on how you must be ignorant for loving such a moronic film. You know these people, they're Internet a-holes.

I wanted a podcast that covered different subjects every single week, in both film and television. I wanted a podcast that featured a variety of topics, discussions, dissenting voices, and most importantly laughs. Not that annoying brand of laughter that stems from a group of guys talking about laundry day and all the hijinks pressed shirts create. I wanted genuine laughs from hearing "regular guys" who are just as informed as any film critic

I put in the legwork; hours upon hours of research and planning for a successful podcast launch. Rob was back to work with me on the website design, my brother-in-law Dustin worked up a perfect logo. Scott agreed to join in as co-host, and both he and my close friend Brian helped me flesh out the basics of what I wanted to do. We held auditions of sorts and Justin was brought on as the fourth chair. This thing was ready to go, and I prepared for the onslaught of inevitable fame, wealth and strippergrams. We launched *The Hollywood Outsider*!

Everyone who has ever begun a podcast knows this moment and every single one of us has experienced a different result. For those of you that don't, allow me to elaborate. I knew we had something special, and I believed wholeheartedly I had chosen the right direction for this show. As we rolled through those first few months though, I started my internal debate: either I was wrong, or maybe I just wasn't meant for this.

In the first year, we might have had 60 listeners an episode on average. 60. Between 4 hosts, I'm pretty sure that equaled out to 58 people we knew and 2 guys waiting for a bus somewhere. WHY would we bother continuing? In hindsight, I honestly don't know. I was becoming more and more disillusioned. The thing is, I was still enjoying the hell out of it.

I was finally able to discuss film and TV the way I always had wanted to, with people who felt the same, and we all wanted to continue. 60 became 100, which became 500, which eventually led to thousands who every week kept coming back just to hear our random thoughts and jovial tone. Studios began sending us screeners and publicists began asking for interview time. More and more shows like ours began popping up, a few I can directly point a finger at and say I knew where they first got their idea or even their format. Some people might be offended. I was humbled.

The Hollywood Outsider was a success, and it was on my own terms. This breadcrumb of an idea, one that had failed in previous iterations, was now a living, breathing entity. And what's more, it stood on its own. It was never about making money, even though everyone thought that's where I should go. I always wanted an outlet for fans like myself that wasn't designed and sold by corporate entities. It wasn't fighting "The Man" anymore for me; it was solely about protecting my creation.

This show also bred other successes. Scott was able to pool HO fans to help launch a gaming podcast spin-off, finally fulfilling his own dream. Justin, as an author, sold countless books to supportive fans of the podcast. Through the show, I made lifetime friends like Troy and Wayne, who I launched other podcasts with (*The Blacklist Exposed, Beyond Westworld*), and even combined with Brian, Wayne, and Troy to begin yet another podcast dream with *Remake This Movie RIGHT!* I was even able to ultimately achieve another personal goal as a writer through my latest endeavor, *Smirk*. With two fellow authors and myself, we write and discuss a new story every single week. These are the opportunities podcasts create.

Through it all, there have been numerous ups-and-downs. If you do anything with friends long enough, you will fight. If there is a closeness, you will recover and endure, if not, it spirals into a descent of hell. As the creator, I do take a hardened focus on every aspect and spend an exorbitant amount of free time monitoring every detail. That can be taxing on others who just want to have a good time. Podcasting is much like any other form of entertainment; you never know the stress of it until you do it, and if you care enough to do it well, there will always be struggle.

Throughout these many years, I believe I've seen it all. Hosts have now come and gone, new hosts John and Amanda have joined the fray forcing this creator to reexamine his own vision, and success is always on the cusp of failure. I have made and lost friends, offended some and touched others, and every once in a while a bad show hits the airwaves. If you do this religiously, nothing hits you in the gut harder than those. Many times, I have even thought about hanging it up before it becomes a bad joke, no one wants to be the Pauly Shore of podcasting. Not even Pauly Shore.

I've also grown tired at times. Some of those downs wear on me, and the time commitment can truly affect your personal space. Each week, you have to remind your family and friends that you will be talking to someone else for a couple of hours so please don't disturb me. Think about that; you're telling those that love you most that you need them to, "shhh" so you can talk to your Internet friends. Sometimes it makes even me wonder, why do I bother?

Which brings me back to my original quandary: why? Honestly, I've achieved success, more than I ever imagined. I have made friendships to carry me on for the next few decades. Why do I keep spending so much of my time on this glorified hobby of mine?

To answer that, I think back to the memories this endeavor has created. I remember just starting out expecting greatness, then crashing to Earth when I realized I had a long way to go. I remember fighting with my podcast hosts, shaking the pillars of heaven type fights, and then going on to record an episode that brought our fans to tears. I remember recording a live episode with Troy in Las Vegas and talking with fans who drove hundreds of miles just to say hi.

I remember our nominations and eventual wins at the Podcast Awards and Podcast Movement, and the sense of pride that illuminated my being. I remember joining *Rotten Tomatoes* as a legitimate film critic, all the years covering SXSW, San Diego Comic-Con and other events, and those experiences as well as meeting up with listeners that I could talk to for hours. I remember hosting the cast and crew of *The Blacklist* and *Cobra Kai* for panels at Chicago's C2E2 and realizing how far outside of my comfort zone I've come, and that I really can do this. This podcast has lead to meeting filmmakers I admire, visiting sets, and even mutual respect from peers in this field, like so many in this book, who are nothing short of pioneers.

Most of all, I remember receiving a letter from a fan telling us how his mother had just passed away. And as he journeyed from place to place, simply trying to make it through the day, he continuously played *The Hollywood Outsider* to alleviate his stress and get him to the next moment. I remember how we created something that could touch another so much, it would push him through one of the most traumatic times in his life. How my mother was the inspiration for all of this, and it ultimately played some small part in this man saying goodbye to his own.

So if you're asking, "Why I do this crazy thing we call podcasting?", THAT guy is every reason why.

Aaron B. Peterson has appeared as a host on *The Hollywood Outsider, Smirk, Remake This Movie RIGHT!, Presenting Hitchcock, Beyond Westworld,* and *Blacklist Exposed*

Blaire Knight-Graves

I hate the sound of my voice.

Up until six years ago, every time I heard my recorded voice I could feel the hairs rise on the back of my neck and a difficult-to-describe irritability behind my ears. When I hear the voice I perceive as my own in my head, that internal voice sounds like the voice of an adult woman. But the voice I hear in recordings is that of myself as a little girl. At least that's how I've always perceived who I hear when recording a new voicemail message. Without fail, I hear myself as a child, and that child is shrill, incompetent and annoying. I don't hear what she's saying; I just hear the voice. But it's not just my voice -- when I hear myself recorded I also hear uncomfortable laughter akin to any witchy villain in a Disney cartoon. When I hear my laughter, I feel like it fluctuates somewhere between a guttural chortle and a breathy, cackling arpeggio. If I were to measure my insecurities, my voice and my laughter would take up 75% of my disesteem.

Seven years ago I started podcasting on the Southgate Media Group network for fan podcasts of television shows. At the start, I wasn't editing any of my shows; mine was simply a voice that would show up to talk about *Grimm* with my best friend, Kyle. We'd ship the episodes to Rob Southgate, and he'd edit and publish them, so I'd never listen to the recordings. I couldn't. I tried and failed to listen to our episodes in that initial year, but that same creeping feeling on the back of my neck would rise. I'd shudder, and then turn every episode off.

Six years ago my *Grimm* podcast got a bad comment on our Apple Podcasts page about my laughter. The comment described how my laugh was too frequent, shrill and distracting. I read that single comment over one hundred times. There were at least a half dozen delightful, supportive comments by listeners who enjoyed the show, but I couldn't take my eyes off the complaint that my laughter was shrill -- a word I'd used again and again to describe myself.

About two weeks later I spoke on my very first panel at a comic book convention for Southgate Media Group. I heard my voice over the speaker system and felt my heart swimming in my stomach. I laughed nervously with each deep chortle, felt my stomach turn over again, and could feel the hot irritability behind my ears rise like an uncontrollable fever. I was a mess and felt like I'd flubbed the entire event.

The next day I told Rob Southgate that I thought I'd done poorly on the panel, that maybe I would stop podcasting. That my voice wasn't right, that I couldn't capture the right tone, that I thought my voice was too annoying to be recorded, that I appreciated the opportunity but I clearly wasn't cut out for this making this kind of content. Rob sat me down and stuck his finger out at me, pointing intentionally at my throat, and told me to cut the crap.

"I'm the only one who can tell you that you're doing a poor job. Trolls are everywhere, and they'll do anything to bring you down, especially young women. You think you're shrill? That's bull, Blaire. You are witty, you are smart, and you are entertaining. People like hearing what you have to say and the numbers show it."

I tried to interrupt him, but he was having none of it.

"I'm serious, Blaire. If I tell you that your voice is annoying, or that your laughter is too much, then we can talk about making changes or you quitting, but you're too good at this to stop now. So don't."

He kept eye contact and kept pointing at me for another moment, and then relaxed and cracked a joke about trolls. That was the end of the conversation. He wasn't going to let me ruin a good thing just because a faceless troll struck my deepest insecurity. He wasn't going to let me stop doing something I truly enjoyed over my own self-doubt.

I didn't quit. After that conversation, I started listening to every episode of every podcast I was ever on from that point forward. Whether I was a host or guest, I made it a point to listen -- often more than once. As I listened, I learned how to enunciate, to drop my vocal range just slightly, to react intentionally to others, how to listen, and to be deliberate with my laughter. I slowly but surely not only crafted a voice that sounded like the one in my head (or at least a voice that I could live with hearing) but a voice that came with a thoughtful, fun perspective. I didn't change who I was, but I learned what worked about my viewpoint and slowly pushed my voice, and work, toward content I could be proud of.

It's been six years since that conversation with Rob. In that time I have hosted three popular fan podcasts on Southgate Media Group, and I am proud to say that I have created and host my very own podcast about how to turn a passion into a career on my own network called *Professional*

Geek Podcast. I present workshops and events around the Midwest at comic book conventions and educational environments as a public speaker. These events sell out to the point that often people are sitting on the floor to hear what my cohort and myself have to say. I don't think about my voice or how it's being perceived. Instead, I focus on the content coming out of my mouth and the messages I wish to impart to my audience. I still haven't listened to my initial *Grimm* podcasts out of fear that I would continue to sound like a little girl, but when I walk onto a stage or saddle up behind a microphone, I know that the voice of a confident, successful woman is all my audience will hear.

Blaire Knight-Graves has appeared as host on *Monroe's Comfy Sweater: A Grimm Podcast, The Strain Podcast, Television Taste Test, The Twelve Monkeys Podcast,* and *Professional Geek Podcast*

Brian Daniels

I never thought that I would get into something like podcasting. I'm a gaming journalist now and a lot of people ask me how I got into that field. I tell them that I got into it because of podcasting. Podcasting has really unlocked a lot of doors for me, doors that I never imagined opening before. Podcasting has been a journey. It's been one incredible ride getting to know people, meeting people, and just hanging out and talking about something I enjoy.

Podcasting isn't just about having an expensive microphone or a fancy soundboard, it's actually about human interaction. With the way social media has taken over everything, it seems that face to face conversations are becoming less common. The thing I like about podcasting is how it opens up doors to be able to talk to other people about subjects you are interested in. I look at it like going out with a friend for coffee and talking about the things that you care about. It really put me into a whole new world that I never thought was possible. I'm a big gamer, I love video games, I really enjoy playing them. I never imagined in my wildest dreams that by doing just one podcast, my very first one back in March or April of 2011, that I'd be able to interview Edmund McMillan who created one of my favorite games, *Super Meat Boy* for Steam and Xbox 360. And because of this one podcast, I got to have this guy on my show and I never would have imagined that.

Podcasting is just like radio. You have to be able to learn how to use audio equipment. It made me teach myself how to do audio mixing and things like that. To some, podcasting is just a couple of people sitting at a table and talking for a while about a subject they enjoy. For me, it is so much more than that. Podcasting helped me take off into being able to work in the industry I now love. Podcasting was the gateway into unlocking so many things that I never thought possible. I never dreamed that I would have the ability to talk to and have on a podcast Jeremy Bullock who played Boba Fett in *The Empire Strikes Back*. I am a huge *Star Wars* fan and I never dreamed that I would be able to talk to someone who played a legendary character in what is one of the most iconic pop culture brands of all time. Podcasting helped me to see what's possible.

I've had the pleasure to do four or five different podcasts over the years. The purpose of podcasting for me is to have a fun time and talk about the things I enjoy. I don't look at podcasting as a lot of work. I get to have good conversations and share that with the world. I love to engage with the listeners too and I've always enjoyed getting feedback from them.

You can make a podcast about anything. You could make a podcast about your favorite candy bars and talk about that. You can make a podcast about your favorite ice cream and you and your buddy could go review ice cream and do that. It doesn't take much. I don't think that there are any limits to podcasting. Podcasting has done so much for me and I look forward to doing even more and discovering what else lies beyond. I challenge you to do a podcast about whatever you want, chase those dreams, and podcasting could be that key for you like it was for me.

Brian Daniels has appeared as host on *GameFAQs Podcast, The Dragoncast, Binging With B & G, Press Start with Brian Daniels,* and *Get a Life Video Game Podcast*

Brian Ryder

I had been tossing around the idea of starting a podcast since about 2009. At the time, I was struggling with finding employment in the wake of the Market Crash of 2008. I had a tsunami of student loan debt headed my way, and I was looking for anything possible to stave off the fear and anxiety of what was to come. Like playing in punk rock bands and writing fanzines in my teens and early twenties, I desperately needed an outlet.

Like many attempted ventures, I would record small samples of myself talking with sounds and music to see what I could do, but I could never get past hating the sound of my voice. I continued to balk until the summer of 2011 when my friend Nicole asked me to sit in on her BlogTalkRadio show called *Generation Inclination*. Naturally, I ended up being more afraid than I had anticipated as I was mapping out this imaginary audience that was judging my every twitch in my head. Instead, I had a great time and continued to do her live podcast every week for the next few months.

A few months into guesting on Nicole's podcast, she offered to let me have a day to create my own show. My brother Scott, a host of *The Comic Roast*, was also interested and as word spread, all of our friends wanted in. So, after some shuffling, bickering and eventual coalescing, we went live one Sunday morning in August of 2011 with a two-hour live online broadcast called *Who Are The Area Men?* (still available on iTunes - search Inclination Radio).

I had constructed a rough script outline for topics and segments. At this juncture, I can no longer recall whom, if anyone, read it before we were scheduled to begin. With a questionable Skype connection and the bare minimum of recording equipment all running through my brother's aging laptop, we delayed a few moments before finally connecting and being on the air. For a brief spell, we all stared at one another, becoming more aggravated as someone was waiting for someone else to begin. Finally, I blurted out what became the title of the show and the next two hours were a blur of ranting and silliness.

What shows inspired me to start podcasting?

Comedian Marc Maron of *WTF* has been a massive influence on me and the medium (podcasting) as a whole. His ability to channel his nervous energy into compelling conversation with anyone from *SNL* creator Lorne Michaels to radical comix poster artists from the R. Crumb era of the Bay Area set the benchmark for everyone else.

The Smartest Man In The World with comedian Greg Proops is a one-man tour-de-force of lingual mastery and a whirlwind of obscure references that I often forget to write down. *The Dana Gould Hour* is a monthly three-hour dual interview show with strange informative segments set to old-time movie music. It is hilarious, informative and bears much of the conversational intrigue of Marc Maron's show.

From NPR, I find that I cannot get enough of *Pop Culture Happy Hour*, a roundtable discussion of movies, TV shows, books, comics and more. Ever since reading co-host Glen Weldon's fantastic book The Caped Crusade, I find his astonishing vocabulary and intrinsic knack for dissecting the most random details of story and character to be awe-inspiring. Through him, I have become a fan of the rest of the cast.

For more local or indie flavor, you cannot go wrong with the kings of the alt-Rust Belt from *The Salty Language Podcast*. Not for children, Bryan and Tony spend a few hours a week waxing intellectual about everything from the latest movies and shows to wrasslin' and comics, and more of all things geek. Having met Mr. Tony in person and admiring his Macho Man t-shirts from afar on Instagram, I can only offer them the highest of praise.

I cannot say if I ever thought of podcasting becoming a career, though I certainly would not turn down the chance. Only our listeners can tell if we are even worthy of such a mantle. Like many, I hoped and still hope that creating these audio experiences would net us access to creators and other podcasters. With the time we are permitted, it has done just that.

Coming in contact with Rob and Martha Southgate, we were generously invited to participate in this amazing project. Through Demian, we were able to talk to Bob Fingerman, creator of *Minimum Wage* from Image Comics. Through strange luck, we have also talked to others from Dan Dougherty of *Beardo Comics* to actor Keith Powell from *30 Rock*. Though we have not yet been able to rake in that sweet Casper Mattress sponsorship, we have done more than I might have thought.

In 2016, we were granted Press Passes for the Chicago Comics & Entertainment Expo, which was a lot of fun. It gave us time to meet some new people, attend some of the better panels as well as have our own shopping extravaganza. Another great experience was getting to participate in the 2016 Southgate Media Group Podcast Marathon. To that point, we had not done anything of this type in front of a live audience, and it brought me back to the nerves that I had before playing my first shows back in my punk rock days. Recently, we were given early access to a brand new board game prototype that is to land on Kickstarter.

One negative experience I had was in 2015 when we used our New #1 segment to review a creator-owned Kickstarter book called *Andrew Jackson In Space*. Tackling it from a strict reviewer standpoint, I had some harsh criticism for the work. A few weeks later, the creator messaged me on Twitter asking for a link to hear our podcast. I reluctantly gave it to him and needless to say, he was very disappointed in my critique. I failed to take into account the amount of effort and work he put into his book, dismissing it out of hand. I have felt terrible about it ever since.

Who are my podcast heroes, you may ask?

Demian Johnston because his perspective as a Pacific Northwest native adds a different angle to our show and he also brought Bob Fingerman aboard. Marc Maron is the big one, as are Greg Proops and Dana Gould for intertwining cogent information with pointed comic wit. Glen Weldon from *Pop Culture Happy Hour*, Joe Rogan for his diverse guest list and challenging retorts, Eric Molinsky from *Imaginary Worlds*, Tom Vasel, Eric Summerer, Sam Healey and Zee Garcia from *The Dice Tower* and John Suintress from *Word Balloon* here in Chicago. He is the Larry King of the comic book world and a superior professional.

In many ways, podcasting has filled the void that I miss terribly from playing in bands. It also feels like a strange in-road to improv comedy or at least comedy talk radio. Again, we may not be that funny, but I feel like we are trying. Seeing as though we are all rabid fans of stand-up comedy, we have adopted the vernacular when we break on one another. Mostly, I feel like being behind the microphone allows us a mini-barrier, which inevitably forces us to unconsciously let our guards down and just talk in a free-flowing manner. In short, it makes us all more honest.

I am often asked, "Who was my best guest? "This will sound odd because we were fortunate enough to interview Bob Fingerman, Dan Dougherty and Keith Powell who were all phenomenal, but it was the time our friend Matt sat in. We were doing a podcast called *The Movie Roast* and we did an episode on the classic Paul Newman film The Hustler. Matt tends to speak sarcastically and from an imaginary hobo's standpoint. Whatever the air in the room was that day, I found myself laughing hysterically listening back to that episode more than once. To be egomaniacal for a moment, I feel like we killed it that day.

When we first started *The Comic Roast*, we once did a show where we made fun of weird news stories each week called *The Night Beard Show*. Without pinpointing one specific moment (as I barely remember the specifics), there were several moments where the recording was interrupted by uproarious laughter. We were not able to keep the momentum going long enough to survive, but we had a string of fairly entertaining episodes.

These days, comic books and gaming are huge for me. Comic books continue to showcase what is culled from the imagination of others, which, in turn, inspires me to try and create something, even if it pales in comparison. Gaming, specifically board games, is a product of the genius of the designer. When I learn a very complex game system and see the rules blossom as I move through the rounds, I get so psyched that I want to grab every stranger that I can find and tell them all about it. Also, despite my gripes in recent years, music still moves me when it is at its creative apex.

What keeps me going?

Gaming, reading, listening to others and making an effort to learn something, conversation, playing my drums, podcasting, and coffee.

What were my biggest struggles when getting into podcasting?

First, it was simply getting up the nerves to record an episode and allowing myself to be vulnerable to the elements in the room. The second barrier was letting that episode out into the world because, in a way, it makes you feel naked the first few times. From there, it was a combination of keeping everyone else motivated to keep plugging away and growing our levels of equipment on a tight, self-funded budget.

For any wannabe podcasters, this is my best advice. First, research your equipment. You can locate quality microphones and a sound mixer for a low price if you assess your budget and dig around a bit. Second, figure out who you will do a podcast with, if anyone, and be certain that they will reliably participate in some form of schedule. Finally, embrace whatever fears you have and take that first plunge. It can take mere moments to know for sure if this is for you or not.

The future is uncertain beyond knowing that I need to be involved in something, even if just for myself. I toss around the idea of writing fiction. I still daydream about starting another band or writing music again. I try to convince myself that it is not ridiculous to start a YouTube channel. I also want to take a crack at designing a tabletop game. I feel that as long as I befriend and communicate with other smart and creative people, I can eventually worm my way into something.

Brian Ryder has appeared as host on *The Comic Roast, The Night Beard Show,* and *This Game Is Stupid (And I Hate It)*

—

Chantel Jones

In 1983 two very interesting things happened in Utah. The first was that it rained so much an entire mountain moved from where it was. The second was the birth of one Chantel Jones (that's me.)

When I was six years old, my father and some of his friends starting playing Dungeons and Dragons with Tracy Hickman. I am fairly certain it was Tracy's own game before he co-created Dragonlance. I don't know this for sure as I was pretty young and spent most of the time playing in the basement with the other kids. My interests, however, were piqued and I never turned back after this. I was still too young to play the game, but that did not stop me from learning about it and playing around with other things similar to it. In the first grade, my friends and I had our own X-Men team where I was a cross between Wolverine and Night Crawler. In later grades, it was Zelda and other games on the playground. In the 4th grade, I started writing my own stories for D&D and creating my own scenarios. At that point in my life, my best creation was Batman Fights Sub-Zero, predating the Mortal Combat Vs. DCU game by many years.

There was a short time when I was in Jr. High that I played sports. I love sports and had fun with them, but I found that playing tabletop games was more my thing. What I like about gaming is you rely on yourself rather than others.

I played both center and power forward on the basketball team and had to rely on four other people to succeed. When gaming, even though you can have team play, your fate rests on you and if you are on your game or not. I find this very attractive. By the time I started high school, sports had gone by the wayside and was I gaming exclusively. Board games, video games, card games, and any other type of game I could get my hands on filled my time. I loved games so much that there were a few times I played Risk by myself simply because there was no one else to play with. If you've ever played Risk, you will understand how difficult that is.

When I was in high school, I was not the best student. I found school boring and so I was not focused on it. In school, I wanted to have interesting English classes, so I took one that was called The Once and Future King, which was about King Arthur. Every paper I wrote in that class was centered on Dungeons & Dragons or other fantasy material. The other English class was called the Pain and Agony of Defeat, a class about sports literature. Those were the only two classes I did well at. Everything else was just something I had to do. During my 11th grade year, the principal told me I should stop living in my dream world. My grandfather told me if I studied my schoolbooks as much as I read my D&D books, I would maybe do well at school. Maybe if school offered more of what I wanted I would have been more engaged and achieved more.

When I started playing D&D, my dad told me, "You could do whatever you want to do," so the first adventure I created was a comic book that in the end, you had to fight Batman. It did not take long before I got rid of that and started writing The Final Dream. I had it all written before I was done with school and even played it a few times. When I was working on The Final Dream back then, I had a bunk bed and would either fall asleep with my writing stuff all over my bed or would sleep on the top bed so that I did not have to put it away. I am now test playing it and editing it to be published. In my opinion, Dungeons & Dragons is the best game ever created.

When I started listening to podcasts, I was working for the state of Utah, and one of my co-workers told me about *The Adam Corolla Show*. I liked it a lot and started looking for other podcasts that I might like. I found Critical Hit, a podcast about D&D 4th edition. This show inspired me to start my own podcast, *The O.A*. It was an actual play podcast centered around a story I created in the Oriental Adventure. This podcast did not last long because it cost $20 every month, and at the time I did not have the funds.

After ending my podcast, I found another show called *The Nerd's Domain*. I liked it very much. At some point, the group from *Nerd's Domain* teamed up with Southgate Media Group, and after hearing some of the other SMG shows, like *Coo Coo for Who*, I knew that I had to be part of this network.

I joined SMG in May of 2015, but did not start podcasting until that Thanksgiving. What was I doing during that time? The answer: I was blogging for the SMG website. *A Gamer A Day* is my blog, and I'm still writing it today. I think that working with SMG is one of the best things I have done in my life.

I love sharing stories about gaming and Dungeons & Dragons. It's a real passion of mine. The Final Dream will be coming out soon, which I'm very excited about. I have tried test playing it on the podcast, but that has not worked out yet. I also have *The O.A* that I am attempting to bring back, and I have a campaign setting that I have started working on. I am excited about sharing it with the world. I have been to two live podcast shows, which I found incredibly fun. I would love to be able to have a tour of my show, maybe do something like Tracy Hickman's *Killer Breakfast* does at the gaming cons.

Gaming cons and comic cons are the best. I have so much fun dressing up as characters from my games. I went to one gaming con as my cleric from the first D&D game I played in, and to another con I went as my assassin that I played in a 5e game. I am working on doing a panel at the next con I go to, it will be about storytelling because that is what I am good at. I believe that if you like nerd stuff, you should go to at least one con in your life. My cousin and I plan to do a Final Fantasy 15 cosplay where we are not only going to dress up, but we are going on a road trip, most likely to the North Texas RPG Con.

There are times even now that I think that I should have done better in school yet, in the end, I am mostly happy where I am. I am doing stuff that I love, and soon it will be making me money. People always say if it doesn't make you money or make you happy, don't do it. I say you too should do what makes you happy first, and the money will follow.

Chantel Jones has appeared as host on *The Kevin Long Show and New Media Lab with Robert Southgate*

Chrissy Piccolo

If you had told me seven years ago I would be doing radio shows, interviewing celebrities from television and movies, covering red carpets, and various fan events, I would have asked you what you were smoking!! It has been an incredible, very unexpected and exciting ride, as well as a huge learning experience. Of course, I've had lots of drama from day one, navigating the social media waters, dodging passionate "coupledom" fans, as I attempted to gain credibility with the actors, producers, writers, directors from some of today's biggest TV shows and movies. It's been a rollercoaster ride, but one I'd gladly get on again, even with all the ups and downs!

A little background...

I was always a television buff, a fan of shows like *Charlie's Angels, McGuyver, Magnum PI, Dukes of Hazzard*, okay, I'm definitely dating myself huh? Well, I never knew the world of being a Professional Fan even existed. But the dawn of the Internet, blogging, video, and radio exploded in the late '90s and into early 2000. The world was finally accessible with television and movie actors not as far away from fans as they had been previously. I never knew anything about social media, Internet fan sites, or podcasting when I sort of fell into it all. Hell, I didn't even have a Facebook page until 2010 and the only reason I did that was that my friend set it up for me!

I was an Investigator for 17 years, working in the City Prosecutor's Office, as well as numerous Public Defense law firms, which is where I learned to be a forensic interviewer. I used to interview law enforcement, medical personnel, medical examiners, victims, witnesses, to aid attorneys in the litigation process within the Criminal Justice System. I truly loved my career. Unfortunately, I had to leave it due to medical issues and I went through some tough times. However, they say out of adversity comes strength and unexpected journeys.

I had been a soap opera fan since I was twelve years old, watching *Days of Our Lives*, then later *General Hospital*, and this is how my road to radio began...

I was a huge fan of Nathan Parsons and Lexi Ainsworth, who played Ethan Lovett and Kristina Davis on *General Hospital*. It wasn't until 2010 that I started looking one day on the Internet to see if other fans loved them as I did. I found one site and started talking to the fans on the chatbox every day, and made a bunch of "Ethina" (smush word for Ethan and Kristina) friends. Then one day, the site disappeared! Everyone was in a panic, calling me, texting me, asking what happened. I was sad to find out the owner of the site decided to call it quits and deleted it a week before new Ethina scenes were coming out!

Although I had never created a website in my life, nor had any idea how to even go about doing it, I decided to take it on. One of the girls from the other fansite gave me the template and I literally had to learn how to code myself. After a rough week, I was able to get *Reluctant Heart* up and running, with the help of some of my fellow Ethina fans. It became one of the busiest Ethina sites on the net. Every day we'd all commence at 2:00 p.m. to watch *General Hospital* in the chatbox, fans would update the site with news, their fan videos, fan-fiction. It was such positive, fun spot. It was one of the most special experiences I've had.

One day out of the blue I got a message on Facebook from Jim Warren. I had no idea who this was, but learned he was a photographer the soap opera networks used. He had heard about my site, yet saw I didn't have many pictures of Nathan and Lexi and offered to send me some. It was something that I don't believe happens very often, because fan boards are just that, for fans. As the weeks progressed, Ethina fans started tweeting Lexi Ainsworth about the site and she started following me on twitter and tweeting with me. Then, another shocker was when I got a knock on my door, and I received an autographed photo of Nathan Parsons. He also sent me a voicemail message, and Jim Warren sent me a photo of Nathan looking at my site. This was unprecedented! Both Nathan and Lexi supported the site. It was such an incredible moment, and I felt honored.

I made the trek to Los Angeles to cover 'General Hospital Fan Club Weekend' for the website and was able to meet Jim Warren, as well as, Lexi Ainsworth. I asked how she found out about my site and she said people kept telling her how great it was, that it was a positive website. She loved it!

You're probably wondering when my plunge into podcasting came? After such an incredibly fun nine-month run supporting Nathan and Lexi, it all came crashing down when Lexi was fired. According to Jill Farren Phelps (GH ex-Executive Producer), Lexi "looked too young and they needed someone who could fill out a dress." Talk about discrimination! The girls on *Reluctant Heart* were devastated and all of us commiserated, knowing her final scenes with Nathan were coming up.

This is going to sound weird, but it's part of the story so here goes. I had been thinking about doing a radio show for a while, though I had no idea really how to go about doing it. A phrase kept popping up in my head, "Build it, they will come." I know, I know, it's from that movie *Field of Dreams*. All I can say is that I heard that phrase for months before I started doing the radio show. Was it referring to that? I don't know. Am I crazy? Maybe a little bit! LOL

Anyway, I found Blogtalk Radio and one of my friends from *Reluctant Heart*, Dania Padron, said she had done it before. That is how *RHeart Radio, The Fan's Voice* was born.

It was created mainly so the girls from the board could call in, talk about everything and they could be heard. On November 5, 2011, we aired our 'Salute to Lexi Ainsworth' on RHeart Radio. We started taking calls, and to our surprise, she called in to say thank you for all of our support! It was an incredible moment and my first interview with an actor. She is a classy young woman, who appreciates her fans and I will forever be grateful to her and Nathan Parsons for their support of *Reluctant Heart*.

That's how I began doing radio. I was very lucky because I already had a fan base that would tune in thanks to my fansite. I think it's also important to note that because I had my fansite, I met a lot of soap fans and began listening to a couple of popular Blogtalk hosts, including Silas Kain, who at the time had a fairly big audience. I would participate in the chatbox, which is how I met other soap fans and I even called into his show a few times. When I told him I was thinking of starting my own show, he encouraged me, especially as several soap operas (*All My Children, One Life to Live*) were getting canceled. Due to this, I had his support and fans that listened to his show, would listen to mine.

Another thing I was involved in was the 'Save the Soap Genre' campaign, which RHeart Radio became an integral part of, as we directed fans what they could do to help. All of this elevated RHeart Radio and my fanbase.

While the campaign was going on, the *Reluctant Heart* fan board was still up and running, although Lexi was gone, Nathan was still there. We continued to support *General Hospital* and RHeart Radio kept going strong.

I also began writing for *Blogcritics Magazine* (an online publication), posting about General Hospital, and then I started posting for *Web Series Today* (an online publication). This also helped people find the radio show, to build my audience.

The next hurdle was how to get some of the actors from *General Hospital* on my radio show? I found IMDB Pro, a site that lists the agents/managers that represent actors. I started emailing several and continued doing my radio every week. When it was announced that Tristan Rogers (Robert Scorpio) was returning to the show, we decided to do a tribute to the Scorpio's. I had emailed McCullough's agent, as well as Finola Hughes and Tristan Rogers, though never heard back. I'll never forget when four hours before we were to air; I get an email from Tristan Roger's agent that he'd like to come on my show. (To give a little perspective of who he is, he was on *General Hospital* in its heyday a part of the classic Luke and Laura storylines of the late '70s and early '80s. He's considered soap royalty like Tony Geary and Genie Francis.) I was excited, nervous, and honestly, a little freaked out. I remember my co-host Dania tried to calm me down, as we scrambled to change the outline to accommodate the new development.

Needless to say, I do not fully remember the interview. I had to go back and listen to it later because I was so much in the moment. I do recall he was very forthcoming and candid, which I didn't expect. This is how I began to book soap opera actors on RHeart Radio. We did a full *General Hospital* 50th Anniversary series that began in September 2012 to April 2013 and most everyone on the show, including Genie Francis (Laura Spencer), Maurice Bernard (Sonny Corinthos), Jackie Zeman (Bobbie Spencer), Lynn Herring (Lucy Coe), Constance Towers (Helena Cassadine), Leslie Charleson (Monica Quartermaine), Kimberly McCullough (Robin Scorpio), Finola Hughes (Anna Duvane), Ian Buchanan (Duke Lavrey) and others as we highlighted the actors and characters that made the show so popular over the years.

Also, I started to cover web series, interviewing creators, directors, producers, writers, and actors, which were also becoming popular. I kept writing for *Blogcritics Magazine, Web Series Today* and then covered red carpet events getting press credentials for the *Daytime Emmy Awards, Indie Series Awards, Hollyweb*, etc…

After doing my Blogtalk Radio show for two years covering soap operas and web series, I really wanted to start covering Primetime shows like *The Vampire Diaries, The Originals, True Blood, Once Upon A Time, The Walking Dead*, etc. I started writing reviews on these series for *Blogcritics Magazine* and whenever they had requests from networks for interviews, I would volunteer. In doing this, I was able to interview a plethora of actors, producers, writers, from television shows like *24, Sleepy Hollow, True Blood, Arrow, Z Nation, The Walking Dead*, etc. This led me to the intriguing world of Comic Cons.

The World of Comic Cons is a special place where being a fan of anything, television, movies, gaming, comic books, Cosplay, LARPing, is highly revered. It is an experience like none other, where your obsession, devotion, and passion can be displayed for all to see. If you are a podcaster, it is the place to go to find like-minded souls who understand you.

Enter my obsession and passion for *Sleepy Hollow*. In 2013 I created an offshoot of *The Fan's Voice, Sleepy Hollow Addict*, with a new website, a podcast on Blogtalk Radio and twitter account, I started building a new fan base. After the epic season one finale, I interviewed John Noble for my *Sleepy Hollow Addicts* podcast. It was incredible to chat with him about the best season finale in television history. Of course, I asked him about *Fringe* and *Lord of the Rings*, so it was very fascinating.

Then I heard the entire cast was going to be at the San Diego Comic-Con. I had no idea about SDCC at all, but I learned it might be possible to get a press pass to cover it. SDCC issues a press pass if you meet certain requirements after applying and it gives you access to the press rooms for television series, panels, etc. to meet and interview the actors, producers, writers, directors up close and personal. Having done my Blogtalk Radio show for two years at this point, I wasn't sure I would qualify. The deadline to turn in the application was Dec. 7, 2013, for SDCC 2014. I honestly didn't know if I'd be accepted, so I wasn't sure if I should apply. The deadline was midnight, so finally at 7:00 pm I decided to fill out the application and a couple of months later I was given press credentials.

Luckily, I met my friend the editor of *Blogcritics Magazine*, in San Diego and the adventure began. I was able to cover press rooms for *Sleepy Hollow, The Vampire Diaries, The Originals, Once Upon A Time, The Walking Dead* and others, which was surreal and epic on so many levels. Sitting across from Tom Mison, Nicole Beharie, Lyndie Greenwood, Orlando Jones, John Noble, Robert Carlyle, Norman Reedus, Andrew Lincoln, Melissa McBride, Greg Nicotero. I still can't believe it happened. It was so much fun.

A pressroom is set up with several round tables, and journalists bring their equipment. For me my trusty digital recorder, microphone, digital camera. The actors, directors, writers, producers, go from table to table to be interviewed. I had never heard that such a thing even existed until I started jumping feet first into it all. I did a couple of radio shows from SDCC, and several upon returning.

Note: the key to building an audience is keeping up on social media (twitter, Facebook, YouTube, Periscope, Instagram), providing new material frequently and doing whatever you can to get those interviews. However, having said that, I recommend you always act professionally. From the moment I started doing radio, I saw some of the other girls that had shows would openly nag actors for interviews on twitter or Facebook. I think it's very unprofessional to do it that way and it reflects badly on your credibility. The best way to do it is to get an account with IMDB Pro. It's $19.99/mo but worth every penny. I would email the agents with a small synopsis of who I was, what my radio show was about, and I provided links to previous episodes to give them an idea of what it was like.

Since covering SDCC two years in a row, I've covered PaleyFest, NYCC twice and various film screenings through 2017. My favorite series, *Sleepy Hollow*, has been canceled and I'm still trying to deal with that. I spent most of 2016-2017 covering it and I can't say enough about the entire cast, the writers, and producers. They also supported *Sleepy Hollow Addicts* and I co-hosted the *Headless Podcast* on Southgate Media Group with Zach Hare the last two seasons. We interviewed John Noble (Henry Parrish), Lyndie Greenwood (Jenny Mills), Zach Appelman (Joe Corbin), Kamar de los Reyes (Jobe) and I covered the press room at NYCC as well. I also have another podcast on Southgate *X-Files Addict*, where we covered Season 10 and interviewed William B. Davis (Cigarette Smoking Man), as well as Lone Gunman Dean Haglund (Langley). It was awesome to chat with them and get their perspective on the series.

My advice to you is to use your personality when tweeting or posting on social media. If people see who you are, they will be more likely to follow and begin to trust your news and information. Over the last 4-5 years, I live-tweet when I watch my favorite shows, and I even had a *Hollow Hangout* panel after each episode in Season 3 of *Sleepy Hollow*, which consisted of 4-6 fans of the show. It was a blast! Doing these types of things helps get your brand out there to build your audience.

Lastly, I'd like to say that I have been very blessed to have had such quick success coming out of the gate, when RHeart Radio now just *The Fan's Voice*, first began. There were a lot of jealousies from other podcasters that I had to deal with when I started because I was getting the actors booked on my show. They expected me to refer them to their shows or give out the agent contact information. I felt this was unprofessional, and although I wouldn't give the information, I directed them to the IMDB Pro. I also had to deal with conflicting shippers within the daytime and primetime fandoms.

My best advice? While I completely understand how passionate you might be about your ship or show, always remember that when you are trying to create a brand, whether it's a podcast or YouTube channel show, whatever it is, networks and others within that particular genre, including writers, producers, actors, do watch your twitter lines or what you post. They see it all and especially if you're representing a show as I did with *Sleepy Hollow*. It can be the make it or break it moment to get that high-profile actor interview. If they've seen you act horribly on social media, don't count on ever setting up an interview with the show. A great example is when I met Orlando Jones. I was shocked when I saw him at New York Comic Con and before I even got out who I was he said, "I know who you are! Get over here!" He gave me huge hug and said he'd been following everything I was doing for the show on social media! Another incredible example was when Lyndie Greenwood (Jenny Mills) and Zach Appelman (Joe Corbin) from *Sleepy Hollow* tweeted a 'get well' picture when I was hospitalized. They heard I had been rushed to the ER and sent me their love. I still have it as my avatar on my *Sleepy Hollow Addicts* twitter account to this day! It was so special. They were amazing and it was a defining moment to learn how much the cast saw what was happening within the Sleepyhead fandom. This is why it's best to stay out of the twitter wars, the back and forth, attacking other fans and just concentrate on what you're trying to accomplish. There have been so many times when I wanted to blast someone or defend myself after a falsehood was posted, but ultimately it damages you in the end. Pick your fights because you never know who is watching!

What am I doing now? I feel I've come full circle, utilizing all my skills, experience and everything I've learned since starting my little *Reluctant Heart* fan board. So much has prepared me for the next chapter of my story.

Last year I switched gears and launched *Real World Witness* initially on Blogtalk Radio, now on YouTube, to talk about things happening in the real world including headline news and investigations, UFO/Paranormal investigations and more! I've built another website, and am working with retired U.S. Army Sergeant Douglas Ducote co-producing his show, *The Douglas Ducote Show* on YouTube. In addition, I'm a producer for *Operation Border Command*, a documentary set to be filmed in early 2020 and released next summer, after an extensive investigation at the border.

This production is unique in that it will be the only live streaming, 20-day, 2,000 mile border investigation with no preconceived agenda other than to seek out and report the truth to the American people. Our goal is to depict the truth about what's going on through interviews local and federal law enforcement, as well as immigration officials to find out what challenges they have dealing with the influx of immigrants seeking asylum in the United States. This expedition is vital as everything going on at the border ultimately affects all Americans. What do they know? Are we being lied to? How is the situation affecting migrants coming to the U.S.? What is the truth?

Also stay tuned for my first novel in the Kirsten Kelly Chronicles, *The Mystery of the Gold Coin*. Kirsten Kelly is a grown-up version of the classic heroine Nancy Drew. Kirsten Kelly will find herself in the middle of a huge mystery involving King Tut, taking her from the streets of Seattle to Cairo, Egypt! What she will uncover will change history forever!

So what's the bottom line? Keep it professional because you never know where podcasting can lead you. Whether interviewing celebrities in person, on radio or YouTube, throughout my career covering television and movies, I've had to ignore the negative and accentuate the positive. There is so much negativity on the Internet and you don't want that to reflect on your brand or your goals. Remember everything you do speaks to your credibility. Talk about what you're passionate about, keep it fun and let other fans join in and believe me, "build it they will come." The journey is worth the ride, especially the unexpected ones.

Chrissy Piccolo has appeared as host on *The Fan's Voice, Sleepy Hollow Addicts, X-Files Addicts, Headless Podcast,* and *Real World Witness*

Cynthia Bemis Abrams

Compared with all other forms of broadcast and online media, it still feels like podcasting is a bit of an adventure into the Wild West. It's a largely virtual environment of small towns, a few cities and a pioneering sense of community.

My podcasting life began in 2015, mulled as an idea for a few months in the spring and my first episode uploaded on June 26th. With a 30-year career in public relations, I knew just enough about writing scripts and audio storytelling to be dangerous. Or, maybe I knew just enough about the process of audio production to know that podcasting was the right place for my perspective and cultural knowledge of women in and of TV. I started my podcast because from my research, I could find no such forum – no place where anyone attempted to take the work of women in and of TV and analyze it, add depth to it by looking at it in a social context, and weave it into stories of leadership persistence and achievement. Banquets and awards, yes. Breaking down the nuances of a performance, story arc or the feminist side of a storied career, nada.

So I wrote a script, plugged in a microphone, bought an audio recording software suite, created an account at Libsyn and took the plunge. In three years of podcasting, I've sampled many shows that pertain to podcasting, television, and film. *She Podcasts, What's Her Name?,* and *What Would Sharon Raydor Do?* spur me to think more deeply.

There are two parts to my podcast career that may get built as *Advanced TV Herstory* continues to grow. The first is taking *Advanced TV Herstory* to the next level by increasing my visibility to multi-platform, namely video, but possibly more print too. With stronger download and engagement, I anticipate seeking and securing higher profile interview subjects, having a broader network of media connections and most importantly to me, continuing the research that enables me to bring cultural and social context to six decades of TV women herstory.

The second part of how podcasting fits into my future is how it will serve as a platform that brings this conversation (of TV women examples of leading, persisting and achieving) into real life. I'm a veteran public speaker on a variety of topics and this is the kind of content that makes a conference or continuing education session fun!

Without question, the single best thing to happen to me since becoming a podcaster is acquiring an international network of acquaintances that either share my deep interest in women, TV, and feminism or are podcasters themselves. The enthusiasm and support have been a totally unexpected surprise. While there are certainly high-profile people who host podcasts and raise the quality bar with every episode, one I have tremendous respect for is Elsie Escobar, a podcaster and podcast consultant. She's engaged on all platforms to advance podcasting. To that end, she's an educator, ambassador, technical wizard, early adaptor to the apps that help get the job done, and an advisor. Elsie's strategic guidance ranges from content-focus to promotional but is delivered in the context of the individual's goals for the show.

Podcasting has changed my life by elevating my voice as a feminist and cultural creative, reaching international audiences. While the finished medium is audio, preparing for an episode involves writing, researching, curating key quotes or messages, reading and thinking critically. Having done this week in and week out for two years, wow! There's a lot to be said for life-long learning, not just of the content I find or seek, but the myriad of tools available to assist me with organizing, researching, producing and promoting my work.

At its highest, most global level, my topic of women in and of TV is huge. I rely on a variety of formats to do the storytelling, informing or celebrating: interviews, scripted with audio clips, and off-script viewing sessions. Loyal listeners tell me they think my best work is found in the scripted shows, where I provide historic background or context, incorporate audio clips from a performance and create a lesson that fills the heart or takes the listener back to a profound memory. One of my best episodes is entitled "The Women of My So-Called Life." It examined the mother/daughter relationships in this iconic one-season series and its curiously abrupt ending.

There are all sorts of podcasting formats, but the greatest key to success is whether the producer has a deep well of knowledge and episode ideas to make it work. People listen because they want to hear a quality show – in this case, quality being both the content and the ease of listening. I am a lifelong learner and my interest in television stretches clear back to childhood. The sharp learning curve for podcasting was a bit of a surprise – not so much the recording part or writing scripts that I then recorded. In fact, I edited the first 26 shows before hiring someone to do it for me. Rather, the learning curve is steepest in the area of promotion. Who are the listeners and how will they be found? If a measure of success is download traffic, then it follows that growth is necessary for the producer to feel like the podcast is worth the work. If fun is a metric – which it should be – then that sort of fuels the patience in learning how to promote the show.

Research is fascinating and fun and it includes and viewing old shows and interviews, scouring the library and internet for background, and talking to women who helped create some of the most heralded, memorable women-centric TV shows. It's a passion! In fact, the entire topic of women's representation and advancement in media has never been more relevant. Women are starting to realize that women are depicted differently than men are in TV shows, paid less and get fewer lines. My goal is to make *Advanced TV Herstory* a source of knowledge, inspiration, and fun.

My biggest struggle when getting into podcasting – and even now – is helping would-be listeners warm up to the technology. My topic has the power to engage women and men of all ages who've never listened to a podcast. They may not have a commute or 45-minute daily walk for which they readily seek audio companionship. A great hurdle remains helping them understand how to either download the file to a device or listen directly from a player at Apple Podcast, Radio Public (for Android), my hosting site Libsyn or my website, www.tvherstory.com. I tell friends via Facebook or in person as I hand them the show's business card, "just go to this site, find the show and press the play button." My second greatest hurdle is having them agree to "risk" 30 or 45 minutes of their time listening to my show.

The first thing I'd suggest to a person considering starting a podcast is to determine the goal of the effort. It is a lot of time and energy – so how does it fit into your other responsibilities? If the goal is fun, then make it fun and a life experience that you'll always remember fondly. If it's to make money, know that time is money and a podcast is just one way to market a product or service. It might be the most wildly efficient, once you've mastered the learning curve. For other goals, like motivating and educating, fulfillment might be measured as much in qualitative or anecdotal feedback as from the thrill of seeing traffic increase month after month.

For the most part, the demographics tell us that those who listen to podcasts most likely never experienced audio storytelling from the Golden Age of Radio. And surely, not everyone who produces a podcast today earned a degree in radio production or broadcast journalism.

The American myth of the Wild West is our way of publicly celebrating the adventure and reward that comes with settling a little piece of ground in an expansive environment. Whether it was cattle rustling, mining for gold or moving settlements of people, the experience was owned by those who simply did it. Ditto for podcasting.

Within my network of podcasters, the prevailing bit of advice offered to someone "considering" starting a podcast – or one who is overthinking every aspect to get it "right" prior to launching – is to "just do it." If you stick with it, the workload, learning curve, and personal growth should never cease.

Cynthia Bemis Abrams has appeared as host on *Advanced TV Herstory*

Dave Jackson

My wife and I had spent ourselves into bankruptcy trying to have children. Our attempts were not successful, and then our marriage ended. Shortly after that, I was pulled into an office and told that although I was one of the company's best trainers and loved by my students, they were downsizing the training department and I was being let go. Six months before this I had won the "Employee of the Year" award. My brother is a saint and said I could live in his basement as I decided what to do with what was left of my life, as it looked like I would be going back to college to get a degree in Education.

A friend of mine came back from a marketing conference and let me know that the "New Thing" that was going to be "huge" was podcasting. I did a Google search, and there was maybe a page and a half of results. I fumbled my way through a test podcast. When I saw the mp3 file I had uploaded come down into this software called "Juice," the light bulb came on. This was going to be huge. It was 2005.

I took a newsletter for musicians I was producing and turned it into a podcast. I rarely received feedback from the newsletter readers. I took the same information and put it out as a podcast, and I never will forget the day I got a voicemail from Michael Van Laar from Nuremberg, Germany. I'm not exaggerating when I say I almost fell out of my chair. Someone on the other side of the planet was listening to my podcast, and he liked it. I looked at my microphone and thought, "Whoa, this thing is loaded." If podcasting were a drug, this was the time I would mainline and be addicted forever. With my training background, I could see how I could be podcasting next to the water heater in my brother's basement and helping people across the world.

Every Internet newsletter at the time said Membership sites were going to be the next "Big" thing, and I knew podcasting was going to be huge. I needed a flexible job to help support me as I went back to college to get a Degree in Education, so the *School of Podcasting* was born. I could be creative (which, being a musician, I am). I could get my geek on (which appealed to my engineering side), and lastly--and most importantly--I could help people.

The early years of podcasting were terrible, and you needed to love it to keep going. Over the years, I've seen ideas come and go. Some of them are good, and many of them (free media hosting) are bad. I, like many podcasters, have a drawer full of microphones. I was the crash test dummy for podcasters.

So why did I push through? I've always wanted a ton of children growing up, and now I had no legacy. I saw podcasting as a tool to leave my fingerprint on the world. That someday I would look back at the history of podcasting and say, "I had a finger in that."

I graduated from college the second time with a Bachelor's Degree in Education. I was 100% in love with podcasting. People were starting shows that were touching people in a way that left the world a better place. It was like the *School of Podcasting* was a stone I had thrown into a lake, and their success were ripples echoing off my splash. I felt this was what God had called me to do.

As I was now done with school, I was faced with a choice: go full time into podcasting or take that Bachelor's Degree in Education (specializing in Technical Education)

---

and get a real job? While I was looking for a job, I was going full steam as an entrepreneur. It started to work. President George W. Bush had just left office. President Barack Obama had just been elected. The banks crashed, and tons of people lost their jobs. They turned to podcasting to see if they could make some cash quickly…

This worked for a while, but then everybody ran out of money. I still carried on, but I took a job as a teacher leading classes on Microsoft Office in one of the largest Training Companies in the USA. I thought I had hit the big time--teaching by day, and podcasting by night.

I remember teaching a class, and a student asked me a question, and when I went to write the topic on the board, his phone gave him the answer. The writing was on the wall, and corporate trainers were being replaced by Siri and YouTube. After five years, I got a call from my manager (who was in Michigan). The General Manager was in her office. It was Friday. I heard how the students loved me, and how I was one of the best trainers with the best reviews, but due to a lack of sales, they were going to let me go.

I was tired of classes filled with students who were taking a class because their boss made them. I was tired of classes filled with students who had no business being in the class. I was sick of being told I was the best instructor they had as I was being let go. It was time for a change.

I still owe thousands of dollars in student loans. I had gone through the hassle of going back to college to get a degree and apparently, it didn't work. I LOVE PODCASTING. I had been podcasting for ten years, and I knew all the companies in the industry. Maybe I could get a job in podcasting? After all, the podcasting space was growing while corporate trainer jobs were becoming less and less needed. I walked to my car with my box in hand. Where could I work that I could look at my friends in the eye and say, "this is the best place in podcasting?" For me, there was only one answer: libsyn.com. There are other fine services, but Libsyn.com had serviced me for ten years. So, while people think I say Libsyn is the best because I work for them, I say because they are the best, I work for them.

I called Rob Walch, who is the VP of Podcaster relations and someone I had known since 2005. I told him "I just lost my job" and asked if they had any openings. Twenty minutes later I was on the phone with the President of Libsyn, and a short time later I became an employee providing tech support. The reputation that I created by serving my audience helps me get hired. It also assisted in my being named the Director of Podcasting for the *New Media Expo*. As I write this, I've spoken at every *Podcast Movement Conference* and been a keynote at numerous events. Recently I was hired to speak at *Social Media Marketing World*, one of the largest events on social media. When the organizer asked who was missing on the podcasting track, everyone on his team said my name. My podcast is my resume to furthering my influence on podcasting.

Over the years, I've started many podcasts. The *Logical Weight Loss* podcast was started to document my weight loss efforts. I had a listener send a message about how that show helped her lose 100 lbs. This was amazing, as I had NOT lost any weight.

I remember a female client, who told me over and over how she hated technology, called me crying because her podcast had just been added to iTunes. When I picked up the phone, her voice said, "You told me I could do it, and I didn't believe you, but there I am. I'm on iTunes!" These are the moments for a trainer that put gas in your tank. They are the reason you get you out of bed in the morning.

It's not just you helping others; it's them helping you. During the time I've been podcasting, I lost a cherished dog, my father, and other family members. My audience has always been there to support me, hold me up, and give me the strength to keep on going. I've never met a listener I didn't like. There are times you feel you're talking to the wall, but when you need them, their support comes in giant tidal waves.

There is one more story I need to share.

I have a segment on my show called "Because of my Podcast." I've heard stories where people meet their heroes, get jobs, visit places they only dreamed of, get asked to speak at events, reunite with friends and family, and boost sales of their products and services.

My first voicemail from Michael Van Laar will always stick in my mind. I will never forget the email from "Ryan" who explained to me that he had lost his job, his best friend had died, and he was sure he had cancer. He had decided since Halloween is his favorite day of the year, he was going to take a gun and end his life on Halloween 2017. Then Ryan found my show, and he heard me talk about how podcasting can give you a purpose. If you have a message and passion, I can help you reach your target audience. Ryan was also a trainer who had lost his job and wanted to help people. He acted and started a podcast about his passion, and suddenly he had a purpose in life. He sent me an email to let me know that "because of your podcast," he had chosen to live. Again, I say looking at my microphone, "Whoa, this thing is loaded."

If you have a message, and some passion, the world is waiting for your show. Come on in; the water's fine.

Dave Jackson has appeared as host on *Alexacast, Ask the Podcast Coach, Because of my Podcast, Bernie The Cat, Best of the Worst, Best Podcasting Gear, Building a Better Dave, Clammr Top 20 Countdown, Customer Service Show, Dates From Hell Show, Feeding My Faith, Grow Your Church Show, Healing our Marriage, History of Six Shooter, Jillian Michaels Show, Logical Weight Loss, Marketing Musician/Musicians Cooler, More Podcast Money, Music News Podcast, Podcast News Flash, Podcast Promo Show, Podcast Review Show, Podcast Rodeo Show, Podcasting For Free, Power of Podcasting, Quiet Study Area, School of Podcasting, Shopworld, Weekly Web Tools, Worst Podcast Ever, The Messengers,*and *Your Podcast Consultant*

Dave White

This is a cautionary tale of a lesson I learned on this journey of podcasting. It would be simple enough to share my start into this wonderful hobby, but I have shared that story a few times, and I encourage those that do listen to podcasts to go back into the chronicles of *80's Reboot Overdrive* to hear that story. However, the lesser-known story is my experiences with "getting sucked into the hype." The hype can come at you as soon as you nail down a celebrity guest or what you perceive as the biggest epic event in your podcast niche that you are invited to attend. What do I mean by the hype? The belief that an interview and/or event will catapult your podcast into the stratosphere for download numbers and/or you will become the next biggest well-known podcaster from this one great interview or event. Do not get me wrong if talking to this celebrity that you have admired or attending that event is fun for you than it is and should be a great thing and worthy of enjoying the moment. Here are my accounts of two separate interview stories that I stumbled through from a headspace perspective in both a positive and negative experience, from an execution standpoint I am happy with the chats and what we posted online. What you will also get is my 2-cent opinion on how to help yourself when standing in the gateway about to jump into the hype zone.

Our adventure is a tale of two celebrities. I am not afraid to call them out by name but for the sake of protecting the guilty (which is more my fault than theirs), let us call them Larry and Billy. Their full names and their respective claim to fame are available in our podcast archives, you have their first names, and you should be able to figure out who is whom on this if you take a quick look and even listen in on those conversations out there available in the history of Southgate Media Group. Both of these started similarly in a very positive manner in the fact that I reached out and asked if they would be interested in participating in a podcast interview. To my joy, even to this day, people will say yes to this. In both cases, I have mad respect for these fantastic men and for them to agree to give up their valuable time to chat, means a lot and I am so grateful to them and anyone that will be open to spending time with me in this forum. Here is my first mistake after we agree to chat. I check their presence on social media. If they have a twitter, I mentally log their follower count. If they have Facebook public accounts, I do the same thing. If they have a healthy active website, then I assume they have enough traffic to justify keeping it going. In my mental headspace, I would secretly hope that a small percentage of those devotees to that person, say 10%, would listen to the podcast when it is posted if the celebrity shared it in those forums. So in the easiest math and simplest definitions, if you are a star and have 50,000 followers, if I booked you on the podcast and you advertised the link to our chat after the fact, then I would hope to get 5,000 of your fan base to download and check it out. Is that wrong thinking? In the case of both Larry and Billy and two very different after-show, interview interactions, one very positive and the other, well, not so much. That is very wrong thinking right out of the gate and helped contribute to my displeasure in one of these scenarios.

Larry is well known for co-starring in a very cool retro TV show, and my interaction with him and his assistant set a very high bar for what I believed all interactions with celebrities would be like. Larry's assistant was uber helpful and coordinated the date/time and connection date and time to talk with Larry. She even actively watched our podcast channel for the link and had shared it amongst all of his social media outlets before I even got the chance to send it to her. Badda Bing, *80's Reboot Overdrive* was mentioned and linked on his public website, his Facebook, and his twitter account. In my mind, it was all over the Internet in the course of an hour in front of hundreds of thousands of his fans. People were commenting on the interview on his website and how much they enjoyed hearing the stories with Larry. Downloads for the month did shoot up, and I got a boost of attention that I was hoping would happen with more interviews I would arrange. This set the bar pretty high very early in my journey of podcasting.

Billy had the privilege of being one of our first music guests and also had some acting 80s and 90s credits. The interview was pretty darn cool from my perspective as he had a small part in one of my favorite 80s science fiction movies, I had a co-host on with me, and we learned a lot of background info that I didn't know before our talk. Great stories and fun were had by all. One of the co-owners of our media group was equally pleased and happy about the interview. After hearing it, he spent his time creating a YouTube video of the interview for our group channel. I was ready for Billy's fans to be told about this great conversation and I eagerly sent the link to Billy along with offering my complete thanks and appreciation for his time. In my podcast post-interview interaction infancy, I also added a note that it would be great if he would send back any info on where he posted our link so I can see for myself and I could participate in any follow-up conversations via his social media interactions. I sent the link to Billy and humbly asked for a response as soon as he was able and then … well... nothing.

Days passed, and I eagerly checked FB private messages and email for any response, yet still nothing. After a week, I assumed he was busy, and it may have gotten lost amongst other things. I rephrased the message slightly and resent. Then more of the nothing. I continued to wait for a response, but it never came. Another week went by, and I started to wonder if I edited the show wrong or did something to make Billy angry with me. After more than a week went by with no response, I cordially send the link again in another message thanking him profoundly for giving up his time for our show and respectfully requesting sharing knowledge of where the link ends up in his social media. I finally got a response. The tone of Billy's response was essentially, "please stop sending me the link." If he was going to post it, he would have done so already. In my head I read, "Hey kid you are annoying me, leave me alone." I immediately got nervous because I am sure I edited something wrong, he heard it and was like "this guy sucks and I wish I wouldn't have done his show." I gave myself a breather before responding, but since I had his attention, I apologized and asked him for his constructive feedback so I could learn from it. I didn't mess up at all; his response said simply, "I don't believe that conversation is what my followers would want to hear." Billy's social media had become his method of sharing his band information and to be an unofficial music historian to the masses. In the case of our podcast and later reflection, my interpretation of his response was simple; he was more interested in sharing other people's history and not his own. I responded once more apologizing for "nagging" him and thanked him once again for any time he had already provided. Weeks later I finally unfollowed Billy because I realized I wanted Billy's history and not what he was sharing about other people.

Here is my unsolicited friendly neighborhood podcaster's advice. Don't book a person or attend an event with the thought process that it will increase your download numbers. I've asked another guest, a very talented voice actor who came on the show much later than Billy, if he wanted the link and he quickly said, "No, thank you." To this date I have no clue if that follow up celebrity even listened to our show but I am mentally prepared now for all guests to not be like Larry and his assistant. However, it doesn't stop me because I discovered that this is for me. I get enjoyment from talking to others about their contributions and experiences. Here it is in a nutshell: ask to talk to people that you want to talk to and go to events that you want to go to. If you like promoting your show, then do it. If you are a podcaster, this hobby is about you and being creative. If you enjoy doing it, keep doing it, and if more people like your stuff, the numbers should follow. Try to avoid the hype zone as I truly believe it is like going to a fancy dinner that has a menu with no prices, you don't think about it and order like a king, you might have the best meal that you ever had, but then the check comes. The meal was perfect up until that moment, and you are now wondering how to pay for it and when you tell the story you talk about the monster check. My experience with Billy, I remember the post-interaction and it is sadly one of the lowest downloaded episodes, but it was a great talk wasn't it? Here it is folks, just have fun.

Dave White has appeared as host on *Banzai Retro Club, 80's Reboot Overdrive, Gamma Cast,* and *Autoexec.Bat*

Dianne Maythorne & Marnell Steiner

"I like the idea that a voice can just go somewhere, uninvited, and just kinda hang out like a dirty thought in a nice clean mind. Maybe a thought is like a virus, you know, it can... it can... kill all the healthy thoughts and just take over. That would be serious."

– Mark Hunter "*Pump Up the Volume*" 1990

My sister Dianne got me my first gig in podcasting, but the truth is my love for podcasts began long before they even existed. The idea of a random "nobody" talking to a sea of faceless listeners isn't a new concept. In Britain in 1964, *Radio Caroline* began broadcasting the soundtrack of a generation from a boat just outside UK territorial waters. They were quite literally pirate radio (now immortalized by the 2009 Hollywood film *Pirate Radio*). They were stealing the airwaves from those who would shut them down for violating regulations regarding "acceptable content," three decades earlier.

The Nineties brought the world into the Information Age. The growing use and availability of computers that connected us all to the World Wide Web meant that you could reach people all across the world in a matter of nanoseconds. (Almost... Seriously, dial-up sucked by today's standards!) Chat rooms and blogs gave way to vlogs and podcasts. We currently seem to be staring over the edge of the precipice, the old world media empire at our backs, and the brave new world of free and independent media pulling us forward. Pirate radio, bootleg radio, free radio, clandestine radio. In the words of Andy Warhol, "In the future, everybody will be world-famous for 15 minutes."

Warhol brings us back to me and my little foray into the podcasting universe. A little more than a year ago, my sister Dianne needed a fill-in co-host for one of her new podcasts, *The Good News: The Gospel According to AMC's Preacher* season one episode 2. I had listened to podcasts, and I had been invited to be on one before, but I had declined, as it was a socio-political podcast. (I find that giving one's opinion on politics /or social issues, to a broad audience, can breed a lot of hate and vitriol and I choose to not bring that kind of negativity into my life. And I'll never understand why people hate-listen to pods and vlogs that they have such a deep disdain for. Seriously, ain't nobody got time for that!) But a podcast giving my opinion about a show, why the hell not!? It was terrifying and exhilarating! I anxiously awaited the episode to be published, and when it was I listened to myself (and my sister) intently! (Scientific fact, you hate the sound of your own voice! It's true; don't take my word for it, look it up!) I checked the Facebook page, the reviews were in, and they were positive. I was hooked, I was a podcaster, and I was pirate radio! Riding on the success (or at least the lack of utter failure) of my first couple of episodes I was asked to fill in on another podcast Dianne co-hosted, *Biters*. *Biters*, a podcast about the TV show *The Walking Dead*, was a whole different ball game. It was well established with a much larger fan base, even a smattering of international listeners! How could you say no to that!? Thanks to my sister Dianne my "sometimes, part-time, temporary, fill-in co-host" gig has become a pretty regular re-occurring role that has spawned a funny little duo we lovingly refer to as "The Real Housewives of Alaska"!

That's my little sister, Marnell. Seriously, how can you not love that? That kid is so funny; she makes me look deadly dull.

It's raining today. My hay got wet. That's the reality of my life until I plug in my headphones and fire up Skype. Wet hay and rowdy dogs—that's my reality until I turn on *The Walking Dead* and get drawn into another season of Rick and the Survivors.

My love affair with the art of the podcast began with a heretofore unrealized adoration for zombies. The fact that I get the chance to live in your earholes, to steal a phrase from a *Biters* listener, is really all to be blamed on Robert Kirkman, Greg Nicotero, and Andy Lincoln.

I can attribute my love affair with podcasting—and zombies—to my youngest sister, Marnell. She now works on two podcasts with me—she's often on *Biters*, where she refers to herself as "the cohost of last resort"—and she and I do a *Preacher* podcast together. Southgate Media has been kind enough to say "yes" when I've said "please."

My sister and her boyfriend send me the first season of *The Walking Dead* on DVD. I wasn't totally without cool; I'd heard there was this amazing zombie show on AMC and I read *Sandman* back in the day. I was unprepared, however, for the impact that *The Walking Dead*'s first cold open would have in my life. I was hooked the minute I saw baby-faced Rick Grimes put a bullet through the brain of Summer the zombie.

But… only six episodes? How could AMC dish out such deliciousness and then torture me for months without anything else worth watching? (I had already binged on Breaking Bad.) I had to find something else, anywhere, to feed my love of the dead undead.

I'm not sure what made me turn to look for podcasts. It wasn't anything I'd ever sought out, and I was only vaguely aware of what they were and how to access them. I sit on the cusp between Baby Boomer and Gen X'er, so my relationship with technology and new media is sometimes wary. At any rate, I found *The Talking Deadcast* first. (Those guys out of Canada are pretty funny.) Through them, I heard about *The Walking Deadcast* and then, because Kirk Manley did a guest spot on the *Walking Deadcast*, I found this little gem called *Biters*.

I still love other *Walking Dead* podcasts, but there was something special about the way that Kirk and his cohost, Jeff Marsick, talked through my newest obsession... they were MAGIC. At times a bit unpolished but always funny and dead-on, I couldn't wait for the next episode to come out. They kept me company when no one else wanted to talk incessantly about what happened on this week's episode of *The Walking Dead*.

At the same time, I was reconnecting with a long time, dear friend. My buddy Todd was now living in Southern California and owned a burgeoning IT business. Hearing others sneak onto the Internet in their own little private podcasting empires gave me some confidence; maybe, just maybe, Todd and I could rekindle our twenty-odd-year conversation and make it into a podcast. He decided to brave the Internet with me, and *This Conversation Rocks* was born. 2015 was a hell year; I lost my home and nearly lost my husband in a house fire, watched our little piece of paradise in Alaska burn nearly two weeks later in the Sockeye WildFire and nearly died in a horseback riding accident four weeks after that. 2015 was also the year that brought *Biters* into my life in a huge way; Kirk and Jeff needed to move on because of their really busy lives (and if you haven't read *Z-Girl* yet, you should) and they offered me a seat in front of the microphone.

I ended up with a brain injury after pitching headlong off of my big red horse, Jupiter; in the early podcasts, I can hear it more. Sometimes I still struggle with words or slur things a bit—it's worse when I am tired, and I notice it more than anyone. Podcasting, however, was one good constant in my life while coming back from what was arguably the worst year of my life.

78

I've had fits and starts—I did a brief stint on an *X-Files* podcast, and I've been trying to get an *American Gods Podcast* up and running with minimal success. *Biters* and *The Good News: The Gospel According to AMC's Preacher* are going strong. *This Conversation Rocks*, the independent sociopolitical podcast I am fortunate to produce with my friend Todd, is back after a bit of a hiatus. Podcasting is honestly one of the best things I've ever done; it makes me laugh and, honestly, it feeds my soul. Because of the pod, my sister and I talk more than we ever did and we would not be complete without Brian (NOT the co-host of last resort on Biters)—the only guy we'd wear a MAGA hat for because he'd sport an "I'm With Her" t-shirt for us.

Dianne Maythorne has appeared as host on *Biters: The Walking Dead Podcast, The Good News: The Gospel According to AMC's Preacher,* and *This Conversation Rocks*

Marnell Steiner has appeared as host on *Biters: The Walking Dead Podcast* and *The Good News: The Gospel According to AMC's Preacher*

Eric J. Scull

As I recall, it was a Wednesday afternoon in August and I was out about town when my buddy Ben called. He and I both contributed content to the same Harry Potter fansite, MuggleNet.com. Though we hadn't talked on the phone for a few months, I fondly remember that he and I had relied on each other's advice in the past to get through some tough teenage times; I told him about my family struggles and he told me about his. It was one of those digital friendships that were very much the norm for me, and I say digital-only to convey that I had never met Ben in person at that time. But we had known each other for years and were closer in our friendship than some of the friends that I had in person at my home in Pennsylvania (Ben was from Kansas).

"Hey, Eric," Ben began in my ear.

"Hey man, what's up? How's it going?" I inquired.

"You know about this podcast we're doing on the site, right?" He asked.

Truth be told, I had not been paying much attention the last couple of weeks to the main page of our website. The section that I ran, MuggleNet's Crazy Caption Contest, took up most of my concentration and I had not read up on this new podcast we (MuggleNet staff) had started, called *MuggleCast*. I wasn't actually sure what a podcast was. The year was 2005.

"I remember reading something about it," I riffed.

"Well, Kevin can't make it this week, so Andrew and I were looking for a guest host. We've got Jamie coming on, and I thought I'd ask if you wanted on as well."

Jamie was our close British friend who also contributed to the website. I had met him in a chat room in 2002 and we connected over our love for the boy wizard at that time. Not wanting to pass up the opportunity to chat with Jamie (or his accent), and to that matter, Ben, I agreed that I could probably make time to record an episode. My summer job at the movie theater was only part-time.

"What do I need as far as equipment?" I asked.

"Just a USB headset, it's like a microphone and headphones all in one. There's software to download, a call program called Skype and a recording program too. The headset shouldn't be more than $50," Ben informed me.

"I'm in!" I said. And within an hour, I had traveled to my town's Best Buy, found a good-looking headset for about $30, and then headed home to set up.

The episode that came of the day's recording was Episode 3 of *MuggleCast*. Released on Sunday, August 21, 2005, it was the first podcast episode I had ever been a part of. The guys and I talked about the recent publication of *Harry Potter and the Half-Blood Prince* (Book Six), the upcoming release of the film adaptation *Harry Potter and the Goblet of Fire* (Movie Four), and speculated as to when the last Harry Potter book would come out (we were only 14 days off, in the end – not bad, for a guess!)

Some things that stand out to me about that podcast episode are: 1) how fun it was to be a part of and record; 2) how nice it was to hear the voices of my friends talking passionately about Harry in new ways, for, we were discussing what was essentially breaking news the entire time; 3) how excitable, but regrettably, filter-less I was in my discourse. I suppose it was a mix of anxiousness and general enthusiasm for the medium, but something awoke in me that day. I passionately responded to all of the theories and questions we were discussing and put a lot of myself into that show. I even mentioned something that had been told to me at my latest dentist appointment the week prior (my dentist was reading Harry Potter to her children.) I surely spent more than 25% of that episode talking. My speaking for something like radio was unrefined. No one could say it wasn't gleeful!

On Episode 4 of *MuggleCast* the following week, Jamie addressed how he and the guys had felt recording Episode 3 with me, right off the bat. "It's Eric's turn to talk, guys!" He quipped, "Eric. Eric. Stop talking, Eric, it's Eric's turn now..." And thus, it was clear I had some things to work on. The struggle of releasing a more concise stream of consciousness was one that I took to heart for a long time after. But both Jamie and I had joined Andrew, Ben, and Kevin as regular recurring hosts on the world's first Harry Potter podcast, from MuggleNet.com. I would have plenty of opportunities to improve.

Now, 12 years later, I have appeared on roughly 700 podcast episodes. *MuggleCast* is still going strong. At one point, there was so much content and enthusiasm for the phenomenon of Harry Potter that I also appeared on fellow Potter podcasts *Hogwarts Radio* and MuggleNet's second podcast, *Alohomora!*, which hosted a global re-read of the series. Micah and I co-hosted a podcast called *Game of Owns* for five years, taking deep dives into the *Song of Ice and Fire* book series by George R.R. Martin and its television adaptation, *Game of Thrones* on HBO. And I always loved appearing on friends' podcasts as a guest.

There are many more podcasts in the world today. People know what they are. It is still just as easy (if not more) to start one, and there are some great ones out there for literary discussion. But there was something special about *MuggleCast* when it first aired. The podcast's creation, conceived and launched mere weeks after the launch of iTunes' podcast directory, was new media in a fresh, exciting format. What started as just a couple of high school boys reading the latest Harry Potter news right off the MuggleNet main page, quickly became a gathering of passionate – yet different-minded – friends who were podcasting for an audience of their peers.

MuggleCast's listeners were, by and large, the same age as its hosts: the teenage population of the world who were growing up with cell phones, Harry Potter, and the Internet. We were the first to do so. And talking Potter with each other, beaming directly into fellow fans' ears granted us – it turns out – a special place in their hearts. *MuggleCast*, at its peak, had an estimated 50,000 downloads per episode, weekly. Individual episodes during big news weeks, or special interviews, far exceeded that number. Having MuggleNet, the world's largest Harry Potter fansite (and winner of the J.K. Rowling Fan Site Award September 2004), as a platform was certainly helpful. And yet, the audience who would digest 90-minutes of audio of Harry Potter fans engaged in discussion, weekly, was even a more intimate crowd than visitors who simply set MuggleNet as their home page.

There were live podcasting events in bookstores for *MuggleCast* as early as November 2005 for Movie Four's release. When Harry Potter conventions such as Lumos took off in popularity (in July 2006), *MuggleCast* was present. The hotel/convention center that hosted a Harry Potter con was a home away from home for Andrew, Ben, Kevin, Jamie, Laura, Micah and me. At these conventions, we would take in all of the excellent programming. I would dress up in my Gryffindor robes and walkabout in the public spaces for fun. And at each place we went, listeners of our show would ask us to sign their Harry Potter books – mind you, books that we had absolutely zero hand in writing or publishing. It was a humbling experience.

I reminisce about our 100th episode, July 20th, 2007, for which we celebrated at a live event on the top two floors of Waterstones, the UK's biggest bookstore. That was a trip that was financially covered through the success of the website and podcast and was the perfect way to say goodbye to our friend the boy wizard. Of course, it was far from goodbye for good – we simply did not know and could not have predicted what staying power Harry would have, and how many future developments like theme parks, exhibitions, studio tours, stage plays, and future film series would be discovered.

Today, *MuggleCast* is weekly once more. It is supported by over 1,000 contributors to our Patreon account, which allows us continually to prioritize the podcast and to travel, still. Whether it's daylong expos in Orlando or weekend conventions around the globe, Andrew, Micah and I have retained the passion we once had as teenagers and continue to theorize, assess and complain. The friendships I made which once led to my being asked to join the show in the first place still exist, and they feed my soul.

Eric J. Scull has appeared as host on *MuggleCast, Alohomora: Open the Dumbledore!, Improvised Star Trek, Game of Owns,* and *HR unConfidential*

Jack Wengrosky

As I'm sitting down to write about my experiences as a podcaster, I think there are a couple of things you must know if you are getting into the podcast world. Number one, podcast about something you know and enjoy, and I guarantee someone out there will listen.

I somehow became one of the founding podcasters in the SMG network rather by accident. I had no training, a Kermit the Frog voice, and a bad habit of pondering my thoughts in between sentences. Luckily, what I also had was a good friend in Rob Southgate who wanted to include me in his new network. You can't do much about the sound of your voice, at least at first. What you hear when you speak is your voice as it sounds through your skull. The main reason we don't like the sound of our voice is we hear the actual sound on the computer, and it doesn't match the quality of what we hear in our head. Brace yourself… nobody really cares. Other people have always heard you speak as you sound and don't know the difference. While my Kermit's voice didn't matter as much, my pondering pauses were noticeable, not only by me but also to my fellow podcasters. I started working on that aspect of my speech (and still do), but in the meantime, I incorporated it into the show. I called it the "awkward pause." Instead of making me self-conscious, it became a running joke well into the show on *Input Junkie* and *'Nuff*

Said. Of course, you will also learn to appreciate digital editing software.

Podcasting is all about having a conversation that has been recorded. Once I overcame what I thought were my weaknesses, either through improvement or by just owning up to them, I enjoyed what I was doing and added *SMG Blacklist Pod* to the list with a wonderful co-host on the other side of the country over Skype. Warts and all, I went from zero to over 4000 listeners a month. The second thing you should know about podcasting, and this is my non-scientific opinion, your listeners are looking for some sort of consistency. People listen to podcasts by subject and may want to hear a good conversation about their favorite show. Actors from the show, including James Spader started to interact with us on Twitter and the whole process was fun. If the TV show is weekly, then maybe your podcast should be weekly. We all have lives that can get in the way, so every two weeks could be acceptable as long as you are consistent.

When I went to the Connecticut School of Broadcasting, I attended a lecture from a very popular podcaster that attracted sponsors. The show was a radio format show that he put out every day, and had each segment divided into a specific outline. I got very excited about the prospect of making some money out of this, but this level takes constant writing, editing, and promoting and that's what he committed himself to full-time while working at the same time on local radio. I am finishing up a doctorate in music, and a professional level of commitment to the podcast just wasn't for me. One of my co-hosts had to leave for a family emergency, and I took a leave of absence as well. Here is the great thing about being a podcaster; it's still there waiting for me. Although I haven't broadcast in a few months, I still get listeners that download the old ones every month. Life happens, and you can always get back on the proverbial horse. There are numerous YouTube videos and blogs about equipment and how to get started, but I wanted to let you

---

know that no matter what your level of podcasting is, you can have something out there in the pod-sphere. Remember, in podcasting space, no one can see your warts!

Jack Wengrosky has appeared as host on *Nuff Said, Trumpet Talk, The SMG Blacklist Podcast, The Bosch Podcast,* and *Input Junkie*

James Wylder

I came into podcasting because I was a giant nerd. I still am, that hasn't changed, but to me being a nerd is about passion, and passion is what pushed me to podcast. Way back in the early 2000's a company called Decipher put out a card game called *WARS*. It was awesome—they got one of my favorite sci-fi writers, Michael Stackpole, to make up the game's setting (and write stories about it), and they even did a podcast about the game's development. *WARS Radio* they called it. I tuned in.

And *WARS* tuned out. The game died, the company turned into a shell of its former self, it was sad times. I never forgot it though, and when another company called Grail Quest Books got the license to make more stories set in that world, I jumped at the chance to help out. I started a new podcast called, creatively, *WARS Radio 2*. I interviewed two of the new writers, and the cover artist, and covered what I could about developments about the universe. Unfortunately, things ground to a standstill in the development of new *WARS* material, and with my own life taking its own turns, the podcast stopped after only five episodes. Still, it had been fun, even if it had never really taken off. As the *WARS* revival had failed to garner new support, so had my podcast. And so had my life. After a seriously traumatic event left me with nightmares every night and PTSD panics most days, I spent the first year out of college being an angry, confused mess. I couldn't get a job because I was falling apart too often to do it. Chronic pain, lack of sleep, anger, and more drained me every day to a waste of nothing. I wanted to crawl into a hole and die. It was at this point that I decided to hell with it, I'm going to publish a book.

I think a lot of people get into things because they are confident in it, because they believe in themselves and their abilities. I wish I could say the same. I expected no one to buy my book, no one to read it. It would be trash, just like me. Smelly trash, like the kind you find after you forget to take it out for garbage day twice in a row. I Kickstarted my first book, and began putting it together. During the editing process, my editor circled a few poems and said maybe I should consider not putting them in because they didn't represent my best work. I laughed.

After all, what was the point of that? It's not like the book would be good anyway. I wasn't the voice of a generation, or talented. I was the kid who wanted to be a writer but was always passed over for writing awards in school. The one councilor told me that I shouldn't try to be a writer because I can't make it, and I should look at a real career. I would never be the one selected for the showcase of the school's future talent in College. I felt alone. Which made it weird when the book became a success, and I followed it up with my incredibly popular *Doctor Who* Poetry Book, *An Eloquence of Time and Space*. As I went off on tour to promote it, podcasting was the furthest thing from my mind. I had no idea my life was going to chance when two weirdos came to my table at Indiana Comic Con in 2015 and invited me to read my poetry live at a Doctor Who themed cafe in Elgin Illinois. I was excited; it was the sort of recognition I had so desperately craved in such a simple way. I had gotten where I was by reaching out to other people, asking, trying to wiggle myself into a dream that I thought I wasn't good enough for. It was a rare thing, someone coming to me with a request to do something with them. It was exciting, invigorating, but most of all validating.

I went to the cafe and the two guys, Rob Southgate and Chris Mau, made me feel right at home. As I read my poetry, talking to them between takes, I knew right off I didn't want this to be the last time I worked with them. Thankfully, sometimes wishes happen.

The first project I worked on with Rob was a podcast called *10,000 Dawns*, an audiobook-as-podcast of my eponymous novel. The idea was that I'd record and post a chapter a week. The schedule ended up being grueling. For a first endeavor, it was a massively overstuffed workload that there was no way I could keep up with in the long run. Eventually, I had to give up the ghost and drop down to releasing a chapter every two weeks. Live and learn and other clichés, ey?

I also started guesting on some of the other podcasts the Southgate's company made: one about the show *Under the Dome*, a show I had not seen before jumping on the podcast, *This Week in Geek, Geektastic Cage Match...* I eventually became a co-host of a short-lived *Pokemon Go* podcast! But my heart was always in fiction and stories, and suddenly Rob and Chris came to me for a second time with an offer that would quite seriously change my life.

The idea was a show called *Tales by the Blue Light*, featuring live stories performed monthly on the air at the Blue Box Cafe. I was hooked by the idea and immediately began throwing together plans for what the show could be like, and how it would be structured. I listened to other podcasts and radio shows trying to do stories, and eventually came up with a unique structure I've always described as the *Twilight Zone* meets *Prairie Home Companion*. Three new short stories by me every month, one horror, one sci-fi, one fantasy, some sketches, and a short live radio play. I wrote up the first script, about 10,000 words, and drove to Elgin to put it on. I was nervous, terrified even. I assumed that everyone would hate it. That I'd be told politely it just wasn't working out, that I'd be sent home packing. Chris set up a literal blue light by my microphone, as I looked over the handful of people who'd come to see my first performance.

"You're good to go whenever," Rob said.

The phone streaming me online had a blinking red dot. I was on.

"In a space too far from anything to be nothing, a blue light shines into the void. Through the shadows, shapes appear. People, stories, wonders, and mysteries...Live from Elgin Illinois at the Blue Box Cafe, its *Tales from the Blue Light*! I'm your host James Wylder."

I barreled through, telling stories, running skits, terrified and loving every minute of it.

The audience laughed, there was a well-earned gasp at one point. I realized up there at that microphone, here were people I was meant to be with. Here was a place I could feel like I was worthwhile. Here was a place I was appreciated. Here was a place I could make what I wanted to, and people would tell me it was worth doing. It wasn't rejection or failure outside of my control like my *WARS* podcast; it was friends supporting me and pushing me onward. It was something I'd begun to think wasn't even real.

I drove back to Indiana, but it I knew I wouldn't stay away long. How could I, when you find a place to be?

James Wylder has appeared as host on *Tales By The Blue Light, 10,000 Dawns,* and *Lady Aesculapius, Pokecast Go, Chester's Mill Report,* and *WARS Radio 2*

—

JB Anderton

I have been a fan of *Doctor Who* since 1984. When the program reached its 50th anniversary year in 2013, I wanted to be a part of the celebration. I am an introvert, and I find it hard to open up and to be myself in social situations. For me, starting a podcast was an ideal way for me to become involved in *Doctor Who* fandom.

I started listening to and enjoying podcasts about a year before the 50th anniversary of *Doctor Who*. In November 2012, I attended a podcasting panel at Chicago TARDIS, hosted by Steven Schapansky of *Radio Free Skaro,* Chip Sudderth of *Two-Minute Time Lord,* and Lynn Thomas who was soon to be starting the *Verity!* podcast. They explained what was involved in starting a podcast and how much they enjoyed what they did. I already knew how to use GarageBand for recording, editing and producing my own music, so all I needed was a service to store and distribute my podcasts, and I was ready to go.

I was listening to a lot of Kevin Smith's shows on the Smodcast network. Aside from the comedy, I really enjoyed and appreciated the confessional nature of his delivery. While I don't think much of his more recent work as a filmmaker or a comics writer, I look up to Smith as a master storyteller and comedic improviser.

Smith is also a partial inspiration for the name *WHO 37* (for an explanation, see *Clerks*). It was my license plate number when I still had a car. When I ordered my plates, I tried to get "WHO 1", which is the plate Jon Pertwee's Doctor had on his car, but thirty-six other residents of Illinois must have had the same idea. Thirty-seven is also the age I was when I moved to Chicago and when the new series of *Doctor Who* began. When I started planning the podcast, *WHO 37* was the only name I thought of using.

I started my podcast as a fan who just wanted to chat about *Doctor Who*. I soon became a very vocal critic of the program. I began to watch and talk about the show more objectively while striving to be as entertaining as possible. My tagline for the podcast is, "Often critical but always reverent."

I learned how to edit myself, much like a writer and his manuscript. Sometimes my conversations would go off on a tangent between point A and point B, and it was necessary for me to go off on that tangent to get to point B, yet I didn't necessarily need to include that in the podcast. I am also not a professional speaker and have many conversational quirks. I was in speech therapy for five years in grade school, and I don't think I retained anything the speech therapist tried to teach me. I think she just gave up on me after the fifth year. I still rely a lot on editing my recordings, but I've become more confident in forming thoughts into words, words into phrases, and phrases into complete sentences.

I never really thought of podcasting as my career, it's more of a full-time hobby. Maybe if I would've gotten into the game much sooner, I might have made a career out of it, but by the time I started my podcast, there were already hundreds of *Doctor Who* podcasts. I've tried making money off the show via Amazon links and Patreon, but honestly, my audience is not that huge. I only use Facebook and Twitter to promote the show and rely on word-of-mouth to grow my audience. I'm not interested in putting more effort into promoting my podcast because it takes too much time away from producing the podcast, my other artistic pursuits, and from my home life.

The challenge I set for myself was to make my podcast unique. I wanted to introduce a "non-format format" where, like *Doctor Who* itself, you wouldn't know what to expect from one episode to the next. One week I would review an episode of the program. The next week I would talk about the sexuality of the Doctor and his companions. The next week I would write and record a rock opera. The next week I would interview someone from the Chicago geek community. The next week I would be inspired by something on the program to open up about a personal experience.

Soon after I started my podcast, I became involved in a local theater production of an original *Doctor Who* script called *The Timey-Wimey Fantastic Brilliant Extravaganza (Geronimo)*. I created sound effects and recorded the voices of Daleks, Cybermen, and K9. I also was on stage as a Cyberman when another actor had to pull out early in the production. I interviewed the cast and crew for my podcast, and I had enough recordings to release two-and-a-half hours of material, which I split into two podcasts. The first one was done in the style of an audio documentary. I had never done an audio documentary before, and I still consider this to be one of the best episodes of the podcast. For the following episode, I featured the remaining interview clips "DVD-extras" style.

I've had a variety of guests on the podcast, mostly local geeks and other *Doctor Who* podcasters. The only "celebrity" interview I've had thus far was with Dick Mills; sound designer for the original series. As I had just recently created sound effects for the *Doctor Who* play, most of them inspired by what Mills did on the original series, it was a great honor to swap stories with him about how we each approached making sounds for *Doctor Who*.

One of my favorite podcasts with a guest was when I broke format and recorded a one-off *Star Wars* podcast with Lauren Faits, formerly the author of the *Geek Girl Chicago* blog and currently a host of her own geeky podcast, *She-Ra: Progressive of Power*. The episode we recorded was a conversation between two generations of *Star Wars* fans that brought up a lot of memories, some of them quite intimate, which was a joy to share with her. She remarked to me afterward that she appreciated my stories. She felt comfortable to be so open with me whereas she is usually not immediately as open with others, and that me sharing my personal stories made her feel trusted and valued.

My advice to anyone wanting to become a podcaster is to be yourself, but be entertaining. Don't be boring.

Invest in a decent microphone. If you're on a budget, a Snowball Blue will run you around 60 dollars. It plugs directly into your computer via USB cable, and it's used by many of my fellow *Doctor Who* podcasters. Don't be afraid to play with the EQ levels when rendering your podcasts. I use the "Male Speech" setting in GarageBand, which gives you a more professional sound.

If you are using Skype to talk to guests, have them record their end of the conversation and then mix the tracks together when rendering your episode. It will make your podcast sound more professional.

Prepare your notes and do all your research before you record. Having to do real-time research on Google or Wikipedia is fine if something is brought up during the recording, but nothing will get me to stop listening to your podcast faster than an unprepared host trying to bluff his way around whatever subject is being discussed.

Be sure you have enough passion for your subject to sustain the lifespan of the podcast. If you want to set a limit on the number of episodes you want to release, that's perfectly fine. If you find that you've lost the passion to keep up with recording and producing your podcast, have the

___

courtesy to release a final episode. Don't leave your listeners hanging.

If you're going to use opening and closing music on your podcast, be creative and original. I can't begin to tell you how many *Doctor Who* podcasts just stick a straightforward version of the television theme at the start and end of their shows. I wrote and recorded my own opening theme music. It has just a snippet of the Doctor Who theme and a TARDIS sound effect at the end, but otherwise, it's all-original. I sometimes use what I call the "porn" version of the *Doctor Who* theme, which I've also recorded, at the end of my show. Another podcast, *The Web of Queer*, has a reggae version of the theme that I really enjoy. Another local geek podcast, *Babes Watch Buffy*, uses music from a local band to open and close their shows. If you're stuck on what to use, reach out to local bands that would love to have their music heard and who will also help you promote your podcast.

My ultimate goal with the podcast is to leave a legacy for when I'm gone. I have no children; therefore, I will have nothing to leave for the world except for my recorded thoughts, my music, and my visual art. Long after I'm gone, I will be somewhere in "the cloud," still in my mid-to-late forties, and still talking about *Doctor Who*.

JB Anderton has appeared as a host on *WHO 37 - A Doctor Who Podcast* and *BAT 77 - The '70s Batman Podcast*

Jeff Marsick

I got into podcasting on a lark. It wasn't something I had ever thought of doing until one night, while scrolling through my Twitter feed, I came across a random tweet asking for someone who would be interested in podcasting about *The Walking Dead*. At the time, I was writing and self-publishing a comic book about a heroic female zombie called *Z-Girl and the 4 Tigers*, and I was both a loyal watcher of AMC's *The Walking Dead* and a regular reader of the titular Image comic book. I was also writing comic book reviews for a website, Newsarama, and since I regularly emailed my unsolicited opinions about movies, entertainment, and pop culture to my friends, it hit me that a microphone and free reign to gab about my opinions to a broader audience was the perfect outlet for me.

So it was with visions of becoming the next Joe Rogan or Chris Hardwick that I replied to the tweet and got the number of Rob Southgate—head honcho of Southgate Media Group, at the time just a fraction of the podcast empire it has since become—whom I speed-dialed like I was trying to win a radio call-in contest. Rob was enthusiastic, energetic, and really excited about doing a *Walking Dead* podcast. The gig didn't pay anything, he said, not yet. But eventually, hopefully, such a possibility was out there in the future. That was fine because I wasn't in it for the money. I'd settle for listeners buying copies of my comic books. Oh, he said, and it'll be *your* show, but produced by Southgate Media Group.

Wait. What now? I thought I was going to be co-hosting it, sitting down in a seat across from someone. I'd be *running* it?

Sure thing, I told Rob. No problem at all.

Except it was a problem. I didn't want to fly solo. The podcasts and entertainment review shows I enjoyed most were team efforts, where two hosts bantered back and forth. I envisioned *Biters*—is there a more apropos name for a podcast about zombies?—being something akin to Ebert and Roper-level of discourse, not just me talking into the ether. I don't think I'm all that funny or interesting on my own, and I'm notoriously critical and hard in my judgment and analysis. No, if *Biters* had any shot at all, I needed some balance lest I become known as "that cranky guy complaining every week about *The Walking Dead*."

Fortunately, I had the perfect foil: my friend Kirk Manley, the co-creator and artist of *Z-Girl*. A veritable walking database of all things zombie, from books to movies to comics, Kirk's knowledge and love of the genre would be perfect. I called Kirk and asked him if he'd like to do a podcast with me, and after I had assured him that he would have no responsibility other than to sit on a Skype call with me and let me record him talking with me, he was in.

And that's how *Biters* got started.

Now, podcasts about arguably the biggest phenomenon in serialized television history were a nickel a handful, and I wanted *Biters* to stand out from the rest. I wanted viewers to watch an episode on television and then come over to *Biters* for thoughtful analysis without having to sit through a scene-by-scene recap. I wanted a gimmick, a shtick that I didn't hear anyone else doing. So Kirk and I discussed it, and we came up with: the good, the bad, and the ugly.

With this as our spine of the show, each week Kirk and I would give a quick thought or two about the week's *Walking Dead* episode, and then we each talked about something we specifically thought was good, something specifically bad, and something that was ugly about the episode. That last one was something of a wild card, it could go either way. It could be a *good* ugly, like a spectacularly gruesome zombie death; or it could be a bad one, like a ridiculous plot point that made little sense. We didn't divulge our choices to each other before we started recording, which allowed us to feed off each other more organically.

Our first podcast coincided with the start of *The Walking Dead*'s fourth season in October of 2013, and when I ran through my notes beforehand, I figured it would be about thirty minutes at best. It turned out to be just shy of an hour. Most importantly, though, Kirk and I had fun!

Even though we were just two friends having an hour-long conversation about a show we both loved, at no point was it enough for either of us to simply say, "I liked that" or "I hated that" as I had often heard on other podcasts. We had to give with the why, and that drove us to examine each episode deeper than just the visual level. We dissected the directing, the writing, the music, and the ratings. I wanted listeners to write in and say, "Wow, you guys really hit on something I hadn't thought of." That's what I want from the podcasts I listen to, that the hosts can shed light on something I missed or help me better understand what I had watched.

Production was pretty simple. Kirk and I connected on Skype, I recorded it, sent the audio file to Rob, and he edited and posted it for download. The problem, however, was that Rob had his hands full editing several other Southgate podcasts as well, so there were usually a few days of delay between his getting the recording from me and then being downloadable. This unpredictability of each *Biters* release became something of a running joke with our most loyal listeners, who likened it to receiving a surprise gift.

At the same time I was doing *Biters*, I was also co-hosting another podcast, *Disturbed*, that discussed FX's *American Horror Story*. On that one, I was with my screenwriting partner and good friend since seventh grade, Scott Malchus. I didn't want the same format with *Disturbed* that I had going with *Biters* because I figured it would diminish what made *Biters* relatively unique. So Scott and I approached *Disturbed* as more of a scene-by-scene recap and analysis that invariably deviated on tangents away from the topic at hand and into side discussions of pop culture, comics, and our high school days. Like *Biters*, we were just two guys having a conversation, and our chemistry helped make our podcast enjoyable. We would eventually add another podcast to our repertoire, *Fast Talkers*, that covered the (then) new Flash show on the CW. Recording with Scott was always interesting because Scott was in California while I was in Connecticut, so the three-hour difference was a challenge for coordinating a time to record. Sometimes we would have to record early on Scott's clock, sometimes really late on mine. What cracked me up each time, though, was that Scott typically recorded in his garage, so there was always some random noise just beyond, like fire trucks screaming by or lawnmowers growling next door. And while I had a somewhat professional-looking Snowball microphone, Scott's was this plastic handheld that looked like it had been cribbed from his kid's Playskool set.

So every week, I had three podcasts, each of which took a little over an hour apiece to record—*Biters* sometimes ran much longer. Add in a few hours for each show per week for background research on actors, weekly ratings, news, and rumors, and what started as a casual outlet for me to talk about television shows I loved became something closer to a part-time job. And that's how I wanted to approach it, like a job, because I wanted to produce something that was of great quality and that people came back to, week after week. It wasn't enough to just create a show and watch the number of downloads increase every week. I wanted my shows to be the highest-ranked in the entirety of Southgate Media Group's library, and I wanted us to become known in the greater podcast universe. Boy oh boy, did I want to be nominated for a podcast award, too!

Career and family, however, can't be pushed to the wayside, and when a personal schedule is full to bursting, something's got to give. I just couldn't fit in the hours and commit like I wanted to, especially since I had plans to go the next step and edit my shows so that they could get onto download sites faster. With a heavy heart, after about a year and a half of podcasting, I had to walk away from it, transferring the reigns to other podcasters who I think have continued to do great, if not better, work with the shows I had a hand in starting. I've still got the itch, though, and one of these days I know I'll be back, probably working with Kirk or Scott again.

I have three pieces of advice to anyone interested in getting into podcasting: 1) be yourself, 2) be passionate about your subject, and 3) be different. To the first point, podcasting is great because you don't have an audience, it's just you and a microphone, so there isn't any pretense or pressure to be something you're not. I've heard podcasts where the host is clearly trying to push their persona in a direction it shouldn't go, and they fail to the point where I can almost hear a sad trombone wailing in the background. Don't do that. Let the podcast amplify your personality. To the second point, podcasting is a labor of love, so don't start a podcast about something, say zombies, just because it's the "in" thing and you want to capitalize on it. Passion comes out in your voice and how in-depth you talk about your subject matter, and it's also revealed in your effort to market your show and draw in listeners. And to the third point, there are tens of thousands of podcasts out there, with stiff competition among them for listeners. Listeners, though, are fickle, and they are always looking for fresh voices and interesting content. So be that thirst-quenching change from what everyone else is listening to and make your podcast stand apart from the crowd. It's the easiest way to get noticed.

Jeff Marsick has appeared as host on *Biters: The Walking Dead Podcast, Comrades: The Americans Podcast, Fast Talkers: The Flash Podcast* and *Disturbed: The American Horror Story Podcast*

Jesse Jackson

"Why would anyone want to listen to a podcast from you?" That is the question my lovely bride asked very early in my podcast life. From her perspective hosts of podcasts are experts on a topic, professionals or celebrities who make a living entertaining people. She couldn't wrap her brain around someone just wanting to hear a regular guy talk about anything much less some TV show. She's since come around and is very supportive of my hobby, but I do ask myself that question often when I'm building an agenda for an episode of a podcast I'm going to host or where I'm going to participate. But I suppose this is the wrong place to start, instead let's get in the TARDIS and go back to the beginning. How did I get into this podcast thing and what need was it filling for me?

I can't remember when I discovered podcasting, but I do remember the first podcast that I listened to regularly. It was a TV Guide podcast where writers/editors with the magazine talked TV every week. That led me to *Ron Moore's Battlestar Galactica Podcast*. It was fascinating to hear a showrunner talk about what happened on the show, what worked and what didn't work. I started looking for all kinds of podcasts and became a fan of *Tuning Into Scifi TV* and *Galactica Quorum* podcasts. It was very cool to hear fans talk about genre TV. I started thinking that this was something that I would enjoy doing. I got my chance when Karen Lindsey and Lou Sytsma sent out a request for volunteers (who had never seen *Farscape*) to join them on a podcast. I signed up, and that was the start of my podcast journey. We went through the series (and the follow-up movie) talking about the show *About A Year Into The Farscape* podcast, Karen asked me if I wanted to help her co-host a podcast about the ABC show *Castle*. I said yes, and then I was "all in." I signed up to talk on other people's podcasts, and I co-hosted shows on *The Americans, Halt & Catch Fire, Game of Thrones* and more. I currently host a *Doctor Who* podcast (Next Stop Everywhere), an *American Gods* podcast (*Roadside Attractions*), and my baby *Set Lusting Bruce* – a podcast about Bruce Springsteen, his music, and mostly his fans.

I'm often asked, why I love podcasting. Why wouldn't I, it is talking to friends about something we all love. I love going into details about a TV show or a piece of music and talking about the story, the emotional highs, and lows. It is a shared experience and by talking about it with my fellow podcasters, the experience gets to continue. I also get a great amount of emotional satisfaction from podcasting. When discussing a TV show or a movie on the podcast, it is always fun to make the other host laugh or bring up a point that makes them think. When you are doing a podcast about a TV show, I think it's important not to just go over the plot directly but to talk about themes and discuss the questions the episode has brought up. I also like to bring in my personal experiences and how my perspective and my history shapes how I enjoy or dislike a specific episode or a series as a whole.

The podcast that is most personal to me is my Springsteen podcast, *Set Lusting Bruce*. I noticed that there was this amazing online community of Springsteen fans. Lynette Corolla did about eight episodes of a *10th Avenue Podcast* where she talked to other celebrities about their fandom of Bruce's music. I found their stories fascinating because they dropped their persona and focused on something they loved. I wanted to hear more stories like that not just from celebrities but also from the every day Springsteen fan. So in the spirit of lighting a candle instead of cursing the darkness, I started (with Southgate Media's support) *Set Lusting Bruce*.

During the 100-plus episodes of the show, I've been able to talk to people all over the world. I've had guests from Canada, the US, South Africa, England, and the Netherlands. My guests and I have talked about our favorite Bruce songs, our experiences traveling to attend shows, meeting the man himself at book signings as well as talking about other musicians that we love. Music is important. Music helps us to cope with sadness, celebrate good times, and help to communicate our love for one another. In my case, Bruce Springsteen has been the soundtrack of my 50's.

In 2015, I spent nine months looking for a job. I was laid off from the company where I had worked for the past ten years. During that time the only things that kept me from being totally depressed were my family, entertainment, and podcasting. I took my energy and when I wasn't out interviewing, I was recording podcasts. This creative outlet made a difference. It helped me feel productive and needed.

A few months ago, I was diagnosed with Stage Two Colon cancer. Surgery got rid of the tumor and I'm now taking Chemo every three weeks to help ensure that the cancer doesn't return. When you are told you have "Cancer", it is easy to feel alone. Your family is with you, but in many ways, you are facing a tough battle feeling like you don't have many allies. Thanks to my podcasting family, hundreds of people sent me their good thoughts, their prayers, and their love. My wife and son were my best friends and partners in this fight, but the support of my fellow podcasters and our many listeners was a gift that I cannot repay. Many Springsteen fans who are fighting cancer, embrace the song No Surrender. I agree with them and say No Retreat, No Surrender!

I don't know what the future of podcasting will bring, and I have no idea where my podcast journey will take me. I hope it continues to give me a chance to visit with people who are passionate about the same things I am passionate about. I hope that I will have the chance to grow and improve as I continue to talk to Bruce Springsteen fans around the world. I hope that I can do my small part in bringing people together and help the world to be a happier and safer place. Providing a sense of community can make the world better. That's what I try to do when I record a new episode be it talking about *Doctor Who*, Bruce Springsteen, *Game of Thrones* or Bourbon (note to self, talk to Rob about a Bourbon podcast).

I want to end my chapter with a quote from Bruce Springsteen (I'm sure you are shocked that I would quote the Boss).

During the "reunion" tour in 2000, on July 1, 2000, at Madison Square Garden, New York, Bruce sang a new ending verse on his song Blood Brothers:

"Now on out here on this road
Out on this road tonight
I close my eyes and feel so many friends around me in the early evening light
And the miles we have come
And the battles won and lost are just so many roads traveled
So many rivers crossed
And I ask God for the strength and faith in one another
'Cause it's a good night for a ride cross this river to the other side
My blood brothers"

If you are a fellow podcaster or a fan of podcasts, you are my blood brother/sister and I'm glad we are here together. Keep Hope Alive

---

Jesse Jackson has appeared as host on *Set Lusting Bruce: The Bruce Springsteen Podcast, Next Stop Everywhere: The Doctor Who Podcast, Titan Talk, The Fandom Zone, Storming the Castle, Small Council Matters: A Game of Thrones Podcast, Comrades: The Americans Podcast, Roadside Attractions: The American Gods Podcast, The JKL Media Podcast,* and *How Many?*

Jim Alexander

As a young teenage kid, I was engrossed with being a broadcaster. Radio was a passion of mine. I used to turn on the SCORE 670 AM and listen to sports talk radio all night. I'd even call in, under the required phone-in age and all. I did my first radio show in high school. In college it was all I wanted to study and do, hosting multiple radio shows at multiple schools (Northwestern, DePaul). Then I graduated, and my search for radio jobs began. It bared little to no results. It's not easy breaking into radio in Chicago. One of the offers I received was to cover pig races, Wal-Mart openings in South Dakota, no offense to that, but you get why my excitement level wasn't up there.

After a couple of years of coasting, I decided radio might not be in my future. This is also the time when podcasting started to become a thing. I had little experience with it. I mean it must have been similar to radio, but it was different. At the time I was asked to join a podcast for the website I was writing for (*The Movie Blog*). I liked my first experience of doing it, felt a lot like radio but more intimate. I bought my first mic (Snowball) and decided I would tinker with it. I got around to it but didn't advance far.

It all changed for me when I attended Wizard World Chicago 2014. That's when I went to a podcasting panel that was hosted by Southgate Media. I was inspired immediately. After the panel ended, I went over and introduced myself to Rob and Martha Southgate. They were incredibly welcoming and kind. I had some small ideas for a couple of podcasts (*The Bachelor* themed and a WWE one). Rob and Martha encouraged me to join their media group and start up on these podcasts. They told me they would do all the editing and polishing and all I had to do is just record the content. That sounded awesome to me, so I took them up on the offer.

Forward three years later and I'm still doing *Bachelor Universe* and *The Wrestling Authority* podcasts. I have grown to love and enjoy the freedom and comfort of podcasting. The Southgate's gave me that needed push and helped to scratch my podcasting itch. I grew from it. Today I continue with my Southgate podcasts, but also added my own. I recently started a movie-themed website called *Reel Talker* and do a weekly podcast through it.

Currently, I put out three podcasts a week. At times it becomes hectic, but it's still always fun. On *Reel Talker* my co-host and fellow film critic Don Shanahan joins me. *The Bachelor* and *Wrestling Authority* podcast I mainly do solo (did previously have a co-host for the wrestling pod). I find it quite easy to do a 30-minute solo podcast, but it's certainly not for everyone. It helps to just get it done when you're solo and get through all your points, but if given a choice it's always better to have a co-host or guest join so you can banter back and forth.

I have had some fun memories that stand out when it comes to podcasts I've done. I've conducted interviews with four *Bachelor* and *Bachelorette* contestants. One of which was with contestant Josh Seiter, who is now a friend of mine. Josh didn't hold back in my interview with him. He exposed secrets and spoilers of the show and was very candid with me. That was the moment where I felt I made it in this podcasting world. The interview garnered mainstream attention, with excerpts of it appearing in grocery store tabloids.

There is still a lot I have to learn about podcasting, and I've been doing it for three years. I try to keep things basic. Plug in my snowball, record on Audacity and edit afterward. I still run into volume issues, editing issues, file size conversion issues. It will always be a learning experience for me.

In today's day and age, there is no reason why anyone wouldn't be able to be a podcaster. If you have an idea, are willing to put in time and effort and spend a few bucks on necessary equipment and software and have a thought, and opinion then get in front of that mic and don't get discouraged wondering if you sound funny or have nothing meaningful to say. Podcasting is one of those things you just have to do and not think about unless you're planning out a show.

I know I would get occasionally discouraged wondering if anyone is listening and if my opinion and thoughts are interesting enough, but don't do it with hopes of getting an audience, do it for you. Use podcasting as a method of self-expression. A place where you can talk about your interests and passions. The great thing about podcasts is that you can talk about anything that interests you and you can bet there is an audience out there for it.

I always dreamed of being on the radio, but with the advances, we have made in media, podcasting allows you to create content and make your own radio. Podcasting is the way to go; radio is fading out more and more. Sure, there are tons of podcasts out there, but I never let myself be discouraged by it. My voice is unique, and no one else can take that away from me. I enjoy listening to other podcasts, especially on the topics I podcast about. It's always informative for me and I have something to take away from it. John Campea is one of the best in the business with his Collider and formerly AMC podcast. I truly enjoyed the Grantland folks, now Channel 33. I think umbrella groups such as Channel 33 and Southgate Media are great. It helped me gain exposure for my podcast being part of the group.

I will continue to podcast going forward as that is the easiest and freeing way to be heard. I control my content, and that's what I love about it. Ideally, I'd love for my podcasts to become mainstream, but I'm enjoying the ride in the meantime. If they never become mainstream, I'll be perfectly okay, having a voice is all you can ask for. It's a simple, fast and effective way to communicate and my thoughts out there on my favorite shows and interests. If you asked me years ago if I would ever deter from radio, I'd say no way, but I have. Now I can't imagine not being a podcaster. I'm Jim Alexander....podcaster!

Jim Alexander has appeared as host on *Bachelor Universe, Reel Talker Podcast,* and *Wrestling Authority*

———

Karen Lindsay

I'm Karen Lindsay, and I'm a podcaster. Sometimes that can be a burden, and sometimes a blessing. I think it's what I'm meant to be doing. It's truly what brings me joy. I've made life-long friends by talking into a microphone. I think it's a pretty interesting story, so I hope you enjoy it as much as I've enjoyed finding this amazing "second life." When I graduated high school - back in the dark ages - I entertained the thought of getting a degree in communications and/or journalism, but my parents *strongly* talked me out of it. Instead, I got a degree in Comp/Sci, which I used for most of my adult life up until I retired due to a disability in the early 2000s.

In 2008, a friend from a *Chuck* television show message board contacted me. She said that one of the members was starting a podcast and that I had an online presence that impressed him and would I be interested in talking to him further about maybe being a part of it. I thought it sounded cool, so I said yes. That's when I met Lou Systma, who became my good friend and first podcasting partner. We recorded the *Chuck* podcast (*CNN - Chuck Nerdposium Network*) with two other co-hosts, Jan Walsted, and Joe Buckley until the show ended in 2012.

Before that ended, Lou responded to a call for help on the *Scapecast* forum for new hosts for their podcast. We were recruited in 2011 to co-host *The Scaper Chronicles,* an offshoot of the Parsec award winning *Farscape* 'cast. The concept was simple. Get two co-hosts that had already seen *Farscape*, an Expert that had been part of the original hosting crew, and a "newbie" that was watching the show for the first time. We'd discuss each episode in order, breaking it down and getting a different take from each perspective. Sometimes even four different viewpoints.

The *Scapecast* experience was a revelation for me. I was already a TV junkie and someone that watched my favorite shows with a magnifying glass at times - but seeing *Farscape* with any one of the *Scapecast* experts gave me such an insight into "how" to watch Television. I felt like there was a new dimension to shows with great writing and directing - and that I could detect the good from the mediocre. Mind you, there's a place for all kinds of TV, but when I watched a great show, I now got so much more out of it.

Through *The Scapecast* I met so many people that I stay in contact with today. Our experts were Brent Barrett, Nicola Wood, Janis Keating, Michael Falkner, Kimberly Thompson, Kurt Armbruster, Lindy Rae, Sammy Mohr, & Wendy Hembrock. Our newbies were Kevin Bayer and Jesse Jackson.

We stopped recording in 2015, but the podcasts are still being released - we were way ahead of schedule. I sometimes listen to a little of the latest release and cringe a little at how different I sound today. Just as I took parts of a previous show and moved to another, I did the same here. On to my next project!

A few of us from the *Scaper Chronicles* had been having conversations about the TV show *Castle*. We were all fans of Nathan Fillion stemming from his role in *Firefly*, but enjoyed him on his new show as well. When *The Scapecast* recordings wound down, a few of us decided to start our own show called *Storming the Castle*. The title was created by former *Farscape* newbie Jesse Jackson as a play on *Castle*'s fictional creation, Derek Storm and the title of the show - mashed-up with a *The Princess Bride* meme.

Our merry little band consisted of Jesse Jackson, Janis Keating, and me. Jesse had expressed an interest in learning how to host, so I gave him some nudges behind the scenes and he took it from there. He took to calling me "The Podcast Mom," while he was our "Bus Driver." We derailed him often, which tested his newly minted hosting skills - and it got even worse when we brought in Janis' sister Kathy.

We recorded StC (as it was known) until the show went off the air in Spring 2016. The last two years were painful. It was a true test of my podcasting abilities to balance catering to our fans and the show's fans without offending or coming off as "Debbie Downers." We used humor and sarcasm to temper wherever we could, and it seemed to work. A year later and we still get page likes and downloads. I made friends with my co-hosts, but I also found a network of fans that became online pals and a community that was truly welcoming.

That brings us to the present. Near the end of it's run, StC overlapped with my current gigs at Golden Spiral Media and Southgate Media Group. Thanks to Darrell Darnell (GSM) and Rob Southgate (SMG), I've covered *Sleepy Hollow, Under the Dome, Orphan Black, Timeless, Supergirl, Gotham, Constantine,* and my most ambitious project, *The Fandom Zone* which discusses all comic-book related TV shows. I also guest (and have guested) on many other shows, which I absolutely LOVE. Not just television related either. I'm a gamer, and I've been on a couple of *Warcraft* based shows, and Lou's had me on *The Stephen King Podcast* a few times as well.

I'm constantly teased about being *everywhere*, so the front page of my blog is dedicated to links that detail where to find me. It's kind of a running gag when I'm asked for my info. My husband started calling me "Obscurely

Famous" and it caught on, now being part of my official bio. I like how much notoriety I get now - which is not terribly much, but enough that I feel like I make a difference. I don't want any more than that. I'm proud of the work I do, and I'm glad it brings happiness to so many others.

Karen Lindsay has appeared as host *on Chuck Nerdposium Netcast, The Fandom Zone, Next Stop Everywhere, Maid of Steel, Remaking History, Gotham Undercover, The ScapeCast, Chester's Mill Gazette, Dangerous Habits, Storming the Castle, Felix's Helixes,* and *JKL Media*

Kenneth Smyson

It's difficult to watch someone you care about die. You replay the moment in your head and wonder if they could have survived. What did their death mean? Even more importantly, what did their life mean? As you ponder these questions, the credits begin to scroll on the TV. You reach for the remote, and with a click of a button, you leave the moment behind - but not really.

That is the experience we have as fans of television shows and movie franchises. At their base form, they are stories that consist of characters and plots. Ideally, both will be well written. But even in stories that suffer from a lack of plot, if the characters are written well we can still be emotionally invested in them.

As fans, we love becoming invested in these characters. We celebrate their victories. We feel sorrow as the characters face tragedy. We lament their deaths. We exist as spectators to another world, where the writers are gods, and the actors and actresses are avatars of fictional people.

Most people might be lucky enough to have family or friends they watch the shows with. But what do you do when you don't have someone to talk to about the show? In late 2015 I found myself in that predicament. After being invested into the Marvel Cinematic Universe, and a fan of the show *Agents of S.H.I.E.L.D.*, I became ever so curious about what was next for the Avengers and their "normal" allies on television.

So, I searched for a podcast that talked all about the MCU. I was shocked to see so many! After trying a few, I found my favorite: *The 'Nuff Said Podcast*. A team of great guys that enjoyed reviewing movies, shows, and even comic books. *The 'Nuff Said Podcast* features multiple shows on the feed, each focused on a different aspect of Marvel entertainment. My favorite show was *SuperConnectivity*, which delved deeply into fan theories.

While listening to *SuperConnectivity* hosts Charlie and Phil I had an epiphany: our voices mattered. In today's day and age social media is a major part of marketing and artist-fan interaction. Take for instance the game *Mass Effect 3*. It was the final chapter of a trilogy, following the player-controlled character, Commander Shephard. The games were highly acclaimed and were a blast to play. Unfortunately, the ending of *Mass Effect 3* was very disappointing to many fans, due to plot threads not being concluded, and the fate of characters being unknown. As the fans took to social media, voicing their frustrations in reviews, chat forums, and even podcasts, the game developer "fixed" the problem by creating an extended ending allowing players to return to the game and have a more solid ending.

The ability for fans to impact the art they experience is unprecedented. Similar to the fans of the *Mass Effect* trilogy, the fans of comic book movies and shows are able to voice their opinions, their frustrations, and their compliments. Some of those who make these movies listen. Director James Gunn has embraced the fans on social media. Whether or not this is good for art is a separate discussion, only time will tell. But for now, it is the reality.

After listening to *The 'Nuff Said Podcast* for a few months, I took the leap and sent in my first fan letter in March 2016. I was surprised at how exciting it was to hear my letter "read on air". Just a few months later I was a guest host, and since then have appeared multiple times to review shows.

I continue to enjoy my appearances on the podcast and plan on starting my own podcasts in the future. I'm an aspiring author and plan to dedicate podcasts to free audiobooks and literary analysis. The beauty of podcasts is that us as fans, as artists, or as entrepreneurs have an opportunity to share our thoughts, our art, or our products. So, if you are unsure whether or not it would be a good idea to begin podcasting, just remember your voice matters.

Why do you want to podcast?

Podcasters exist on a spectrum of motivation. On one end of the spectrum is the desire for income. On the other end of the spectrum is the passion for the material their podcast covers. I've listened to many different podcasts, and not one falls completely to the ends of that spectrum. They might lean towards one or the other, but there is always a mixture within.

Take for instance Kevin Smith's podcast, *Fatman on Batman*. His show is a platform for profit. It's a dream job. Aside from his movies and television shows he directs, he has developed his podcast into a viable business.

But what about the passion podcasts? Aside from the aforementioned *'Nuff Said Podcast*, another podcast I listen to frequently is *League of Geekz*. Hosted by Alil, Sean, and Steve, it's a fun podcast where the team dives into their passions on geek-centric topics. At the time of this writing, these guys have recorded over 200 weekly episodes, movie reviews, and television reviews. That's over four years of commitment. But aside from a Patreon account for funding, these guys are clearly in it for the passion. It's contagious and keeps me tuned in every week.

So what kind of podcast do you want to host? I ask this because it's important for you to know what you truly want. Once your motivations are clear, you can write your goals down and form a plan.

When will you start your podcast?

So what about my plan? Previously I mentioned that my desire for a podcast is intertwined with my desire to be a published author. I have notes and outlines for a lot of material I want to cover on a podcast. So why haven't I started?

Running a podcast is a mixture of money and time. It costs money to buy the equipment: computer, microphone, programs, etc. But it also costs time. But the hardest asset to acquire is time. Ask your average author, artist, or musician their experiences in working in their field. Often there is little to no monetary gain at first, J.K. Rowling notwithstanding. Family and friends can find it hard to accept your newfound "hobby." Spending time recording might be cute to them until you can't make it to a party because you have a recording with two other hosts scheduled that evening.

How does all this apply to me? Time for vulnerability...

My wife and I got married on April 2016. At the time of this writing, we have tens of thousands of dollars in debt. Considering our current incomes, the amount is a behemoth that seems to crush our dreams. But after getting on a very tight budget, and adopting a great get-out-of-debt plan (I recommend reading *The Total Money Makeover by Dave Ramsey*), my wife and I are on track to knock this debt out. Once we have this debt knocked out, my life will open up considerably. Right now I work 50-75 hours a week, from my primary job and driving for Uber. But once our debt is cleared, those extra hours will be dedicated to my book writing and podcasting. I am glad that I'm going through this process since it's forcing me to evaluate my priorities.

So now I ask you: what are your priorities in your life? Take some time to reflect on your present life, and what you want from your future. The beautiful thing here is that there is no right or wrong answer. It isn't a test. It's a time to plan your goals, and get passionate about podcasting! Are you going to be passionate about an hour-long recording once a week? Or are you going to record multiple days a week? It's up to you! But once you find that balance of passion and priorities in your life, you'll be well on your way to being a podcaster!

Kenneth Smyson has appeared as host on *Nuff Said Podcast, A Skyrim Addict,* and *League of Geekz*

Lawrence Burgess

This is not a chapter about podcasting per se, but it's about my story from getting nowhere to somewhere. Southgate Media has been very generous to me and supportive of my journey. Thanks to Rob, Martha, and Molly... quality human beings. I didn't think my story is exactly related to the subject of this book, but I believe it could help curiosity seekers take the plunge. To turn dabblers into doers.

It's unusual to grow up with non-musical audio, but I got lucky. I have parents and family who encouraged my ear since I was a wee little bastard—me in my crib, audiobooks, and radio in the background. Honestly, I remember it.

The first types of non-musical, or "cinematic" audio came to me via DC Comics. The Justice League. Specifically, *Batman and Robin: The Case of the Laughing Sphinx*. It had a full voice cast, sound effects, music, and even a nod to some of the monsters. It was a great way to experience stories.

Thus I began to collect audiobooks, radio shows, and everything in between. *The Shadow, CBS Radio Mystery Theater, Suspense, Inner Sanctum Mysteries*, and the Dirk Maggs DC Comics projects were the most frequent players in my stable of shizzle. It never occurred to me to dabble in voice acting until many years later. I had the acting virus in me—Templeton in *Charlotte's Web*, Captain Hook, Gomez in the *Addams Family*, choirs and operas.

Even during undergrad work, though I took my electives in screenwriting and filmmaking. I thank Kristen and my professor Dave Brock to convince me to pursue the art bug professionally. Films were fun. I knew films. I spurned law school and went to film school where I learned what made bad films bad, good films good, and how to make a story. Note to all potential artists: MAKE A STORY. Don't waste your time (or mine) by just randomly putting words to a page or sounds in the air. It's a horrible practice.

Make your journey scrumptious. I try but often fail. I wake up every morning as if evil gnomes were nipping at my heels. Did I mention I hate gnomes? Hate them. Hate. Gnomes are diabolical creatures, releasing flocks of wild geese into the local villages... killing and pooping and biting with reckless abandon. I caught one once. I then strapped it to a block of stone, taped its eyelids open, and forced it to watch the '04 version of *Van Helsing*. The little bastard is in my person dungeon, watching the abomination of a film in a permanent, continuous loop.

The enemy of bad film is great literature.

Dracula is one of the most published books in the world, and one of the most important. Despite its 1897 publication date, it still bellows as one of the great kings in literature—sex, death, and immortality. I listened to everything relating to the mythos—Mercury Theatre, CBS Radio, audiobooks, live audio dramas, pastiches, sequels, prequels, and soundtracks. Oh my. If I added up the amount of hours studying the mythos, I'd probably... maybe...
Let's just say that my history background helps.

Dracula audio most often comes in two forms—abridged and dramatized, and unabridged and non-dramatized. Why not do both?

Seriously. All of it. Even Captain Donelson. You've probably never heard of the good captain of the Czarina Catherine, and that is reason enough to do it. That was my idea, a fully dramatized version of the whole book. Madness? Absolutely. Worth it? Definitively.

I called up my friend and classmate Adam Stover and told him about my idea. Not only did he like it, but he also became my partner, and took the idea to a whole different level. If you see Adam on the street, give him a high five. The amount of hours and care put into *Dracula* by Adam would make a hippie cry. Over 130 auditioned, and I was fortunate enough to compile a downright criminal cast. From the top down, there isn't a weak link. That's why my *Dracula* is the definitive *Dracula*. That's your first lesson. You cannot make a good production alone. If you think you can, you've already lost. You need people to help you. You need an Ethan Lyvers, Josh Drew, Andrea Jones, and John Johnson to headline. You need a Greg Hunt to compose a wicked score. You need Adam. You need your friends. You need your family. Don't fall into the trap of equating asking for help with weakness. It's a stupid practice. Don't do it. I used to work for state government where little pockets of "turf" rose in the workplace. If you've worked in an office, you get it. That cantankerous old twit who does invoices. The sociopathic supervisor who stalks their employees. The big boss who claims their secretaries as personal concubines. The egomaniac in the next room. Don't be that person. Those people suck.

Second lesson: like what you make. If you can't listen to what you've made, I'm not going to listen either. Audiences aren't stupid. As audio becomes more diversified, consumers get smarter.

Don't settle for a boring take. Be excellent. Be sumptuous, like me. Third lesson: you must have a budget. I went to school with a horde of people who thought they were going to make zombie productions on a zero budget. It shows. I've had colleagues who had clients who expected them to dump dozens of hours into a project for free. I hear the excuse: I have no money. Guess what? Everyone is broke. People weigh whether to buy food or pay the electric bill every freaking day. But you still spend your money on the $400 smartphone and buy video games by the truckload. There is always discretionary income available. If you want to get serious, you need to think seriously.

Fourth and final lesson: avoid the shit. The creative community is often petty and fickle. There will be people who are jealous. There will be people who don't understand. There will be people who will try to willfully obstruct you. Screw 'em. I had a cyber stalker while making *Dracula*. It was not sexy. The woman looked like the lovechild of the big wart on the Wicked Witch's nose and Lon Chaney, Jr. in werewolf form. She didn't stop me; so don't let the pricks stop you either. It will be long, difficult, and frustrating. But the end is worth it. Try to enjoy the journey, because life is terrible enough. Hone your creativity and make something great. Get help and don't quit. You are worth it. You deserve it. Tear it up and have fun.

Lawrence Burgess's production credits include *Dracula: The Audio Drama, Charlotte's Web, Sherlock Holmes and the Beast of Whitechapel, Carmilla, It's a Wonderful Life: A Live Radio Play, the West Virginia Power Baseball Team, Pagliacci,* and *Sherlock Holmes and the Plague of Dracula.* His frequent collaborators include Crooked Letter Creative, Astral Theatre Collective, and the Fox Burrow. He is married to his best friend Kristen, who tries to reign in his dark sense of humor. Together they play games and wrangle cats.

Lawrence Burgess has appeared as host on *Dracula Podcast*

Martha W. Southgate

I am a reluctant podcaster. I began podcasting because my husband, Rob, wanted to start a network. He loves podcasts and was an early adopter of the genre. I'm quite certain that I had never actually heard a podcast before attempting my first one. It's not that I don't like them it's simply because I'm not an auditory learner and my auditory processing skills are sorely lacking. I've listened to audiobooks and five minutes after a climactic scene I have no memory whatsoever of what has happened. One time my daughter and I were listening to a book and she mentioned that someone had died. I was dumbfounded. She died?! Apparently, it had happened, and my brain didn't retain any of it. In some ways, this is fun because everything old is new again, but it can be very challenging when trying to bond with your husband over his love of podcasts.

Rob was learning the ropes at another podcast network, doing a fan podcast about *Zero Hour*, when his co-hosts quit because they didn't enjoy the series. I didn't want the network to have an incomplete show, so I offered to do the podcast with Rob to finish it out. I was very anxious. I had never liked the sound of my voice and putting it out there for the world to hear was very concerning for me. I have found, since then, that this is the number one reason people give me for not wanting to podcast. I see it, especially in women. Please, if this sounds like you, push through it. Don't keep yourself from sharing your passion. I'm so glad that I didn't let it stop me. I was also afraid that I didn't know enough about the topic even though I had seen the show. I felt like a fraud. I believed that the audience would be experts and would have more insight and knowledge than I possibly could. Who was I to put myself out there as someone with knowledge and insight? Why would they listen to me? This fear led me to take meticulous notes and have a ridiculous need to go beat by beat through the show so as not to miss anything while we podcasted. This fear is the second most popular reason that people don't want to podcast. They are afraid they don't know enough or they are afraid that no one would want to hear what they have to say about the topic. The truth is that very few people are truly experts. It's all about sharing your thoughts and opinions. There will always be people who want to hear them, and that's especially helpful when your family and friends are tired of your ramblings. I tried to control the podcasts, but this control that I wielded to combat the anxiety caused me so much stress. It wasn't fun to podcast this way, but the thought of winging it with my loose cannon of a husband was unimaginable. He'd go off in every direction and my notes gave us the map home. Those early shows are enjoyable to listen to because it's obvious that the more I'm trying to control him the more outlandish he becomes. It would be hundreds of podcasts before I finally relaxed, relinquished my control, and leaned into the experience.

When *Under the Dome* came out, Rob and I decided to have that be the first show for Southgate Media Group. It remains one of my favorite podcasts. Our daughter has been listening to it, even though she never endured the torturous episodes of the TV show, and hearing it again brings me such joy. It's difficult to know if you are picking the right material to podcast about and a TV show can be hit or miss, but hanging in there through three agonizing seasons, in this case, was worth it. What a blast! We also made some great friends along the way. Often beginner podcasters worry about what material to choose and bail on a show when they lose interest. I beg you to hang in there and see it through. Shift your focus and have fun with it. Sometimes you strike gold in the places you least expect it.

When our daughter was six, she came to us wanting to do a podcast about *Once Upon a Time*. We had never seen an episode and they were well on their way through the third season. This show airs 22 episodes a year, so we were way behind. Molly's goal was to podcast all the episodes leading up to season four. We started in November and completed all 66 episodes before season four started at the end of September. 66 episodes in 10 months, with a six-year-old. I don't recommend it. It is especially stressful for me to think back on because I was still fully in my frantic note-taking/control mode. Molly would often wake up in the morning and get us recording. Our record for the number of podcasts recorded in a single day is six and I still don't know how we did it. She is hardcore when she is fixed on a goal! One of the biggest challenges podcasters face is finding the right partner. In this case, we were working with a partner who was driven and focused, but it is very difficult when you have picked one who is hard to pin down or one who is not fully invested in the project. Rob and I have been lucky, for the most part, in this area, but it is a struggle for a large majority of podcasters. Have a few people in mind for replacements, allow guests to sit in when your partner isn't available, and understand that this goes with the territory. Life often gets in the way of podcasting. Most people have a full-time job and family pressures. Try batch recording. You can record several podcasts at once so that you have a reserve for weeks where you can't record. Be flexible and have good communication with your partner. Podcasting is about more than just the content. Build relationships.

Southgate Media Group started doing live podcasts in 2014 and that brought my greatest fears to the forefront. I had fears of public speaking, being filmed, and putting myself out in the world for criticism. I now do all those things quite effortlessly. I am an entrepreneur and I'm sure that the distraction of building something and filling the time made me forget that I was doing all those things that scared me. I didn't have to go up alone which made a huge difference. I was going to make a fool of myself, but others would be doing the same thing. I forgot the cameras were going after a while and if I never had to see the footage, I could pretend it didn't exist. Rob and I have always created content that we felt our friends would enjoy. We have never done it to build an audience or for outside accolades. If our friends think it's funny, that is all that matters. Live performing challenged that a bit. We weren't sitting up there staring at our friends. We were staring at strangers and often people who weren't there to watch us perform…they just wanted a sandwich. It is very difficult to create new content and perform it for people who aren't interested and are talking over you. We did it anyway. Week after week, for two years. We eventually got burnt out trying to come up with fresh new content for three hours every Saturday night, so we went to a once a month format. It is now an event and less frequent, so people are more inclined to come. If you're a beginning podcaster or a seasoned podcaster, try to do a live event. Join a panel at a convention. Podcast at a coffee shop. Do live interviews. Get out of your basement and challenge yourself to go in front of a live audience…even if it's just three people. It will help you grow in ways you can't imagine.

I didn't choose the pod life, it chose me, but it has shaped me and given me a platform to grow, unlike anything I have ever done in my life. It has given me a community beyond any that I could have ever dreamed of. It has forced me to face my biggest fears and see that I am capable of so much more than the box I put myself in. Podcasting has given me opportunities to perform, write, travel, meet people, and create. It feeds my love of networking, entrepreneurship, marketing, and geek and pop culture. It is so much more than talking into a microphone about our favorite subjects. It seeps into every area of life and, when we allow it to, it changes us. Podcasting wasn't my dream, but it has become my dream fulfilled.

"Be brave enough to travel the unknown path, and learn what you are capable of." ~ *Rachel Wolchin*

Martha W. Southgate has appeared as a host on *Broken to Brave, Ever After: The Once Upon a Time Podcast, Coo Coo for Who, Live at the Blue Box, Pinheads, Orange is the New Black Podcast, Chester's Mill Report, Zero Hour, Maybe Not the Worst Podcast Ever, Ever After in Wonderland, Counter Culture, Binge Worthy, Input Junkie, The Killing Podcast, Pop Culture Countdown,* and *Reel Idiots*

Melissa Maxey

I started podcasting in September of 2013. My partner, Lauren, and I had just finished doing some stuff for *The Killing* television series. They had canceled the series, and so I was looking for something that I would be able to do that would be interesting. My partner was doing something different at the time so I wanted to do something, too. SMG had put a call out for someone to do a podcast for *The Blacklist* television series. I got that feeling where you know something exciting is going to happen, or maybe something is going to change in your life, and you get chills. I immediately contacted Rob at SMG and said, "I would love to do that because I think the series is going to be popular, and take off." That's how I started podcasting. I'd never done anything like that before. I'm not someone who's going to be the one to volunteer to stand up in front of a crowd and talk about anything. I'm the one that's going to sit in the background and listen and maybe write something down as an interjection, but not someone who's going to be like, yeah, this is me, this is what I want to do. So, choosing to do the podcast was a huge step for me because I was never that person that was able to do something like that.

I hadn't listened to podcasts. I watched TV and movies and I read books, but I never actually listened to audiobooks or listened to podcasts before. So, that was new too, because I was introduced to a whole new world of entertainment.

I'm a huge *X-Files* fan and back when it first aired, we didn't have the capability of talking about the shows that we loved except via chat groups. It would have been an interesting thing to be able to do back then, to talk about our favorite shows like *The X-Files*. And then SMG started doing a podcast on *The Killing*, which was kind of funny because Lauren and I had talked about doing the same thing when we had started our social media stuff. And we're like, oh, well, Rob's already started it. So, we'll just connect with them and be able to include some of their stuff on our social media. So that was kind of how we got started and thinking about podcasting. We were thinking, "Oh my gosh, this is a whole new avenue that's kind of break out. To be able to talk about shows that we love and reach a whole new audience."

When Jack and I started podcasting, we were the first ones that were podcasting about that show. We got a lot of feedback from *The Blacklist*, the producers, etc. because we would tweet with them online too, we wouldn't just podcast, we would actually engage with the cast and the crew, and the fans. We had moments where we were called out by the producer of the show, and by some of the actors. It was one of the first tweet sessions that we were doing with the series when James Spader called me out on a tweet. He said something about me being in Boise, Idaho, and something funny about the city. I was blown away that he had been listening to our podcast, and listening to what we had been saying. That was where it took me to the next level. I thought, oh my gosh, for someone who has been in acting for decades, to be able to connect with someone like me was amazing. Those are the moments that I look for when we're podcasting. It is being able to interact with the cast and crews of shows, and also with the fans. And we've had a lot of success with that.

Podcasting has changed my life because it's given me a whole new idea of what I can do. Because I'm still at a point where I'm wondering, "What am I going to do with my life? What do I want to do?" And podcasting was something that I didn't expect that I could be a part of. It branches me out further than just my little home state, my little hometown, and I can work with people that don't live next to me and we can do it over the airwaves. That was truly enlightening for me. Jack and I had a really good interaction between us. And it was as if we were brother and sister sitting on our couch watching the show together and then talking about it.

Lauren, my best friend and partner with *The Killing*, passed away and it really threw me down the rabbit hole because it tore my life apart. I think what keeps me going is the idea that it's about connections, right? It's about connecting with people, that's why I'm here. Otherwise, there wouldn't be any purpose to life, and that's something that has been poignant with me since her death. Because when your best friend passes away, there's this big hole. It's not like I'm simply trying to fill the hole. I want to feel like I'm connecting with people. Podcasting is a way to connect with people, even though I'm not directly talking with a person who's listening to my podcast.

The advice I would give is to find people who are podcasting and ask them questions. Find out how they're doing it, what equipment they use, and what ways you can do it economically. Ask how you get your podcast out there to the world. It's all about community, so you want to find people to record with who are going to be a good fit for you, that you could talk with, and feel comfortable.

Melissa Maxey has appeared as host on *The SMG Blacklist Podcast* and *Bosch Podcast*

Michelle Lynn

In the spring of 2015, I was spending most of my time just trying to keep it together. I had recently ended a long-term relationship, and I found myself struggling through the adjustment of living alone, being a single mom, and figuring out if I could do any of this on my own. It was probably the loneliest and scariest time of my adult life, and starting a podcast was the furthest thing from my mind. The universe, however, has a magical way of helping you find the things in life that you don't even know you need, and that's what happened for me with Brian "The Captain" Kovacs and his podcast *The Captain's Pod*.

I met Brian at the tail end of my failing marriage in 2014. A mutual friend saw a picture of my daughter and I dressed as a Dalek and Tardis on Facebook, and this friend decided to mention Brian's name in the comment section of my post. Knowing that Brian adores anything *Doctor Who*, this friend was certain he would also enjoy my photo. Once he was notified, Brian and I had to become friends in order for him to view anything on my page. I can't be certain, but it is possible all of this was just a ploy constructed by our dear friend for the two of us to meet one another. Regardless of initial intentions, we did connect, converse, and quickly form a mutual bond over our shared interests and experiences. It was Brian's honesty and willingness to have deep, meaningful conversations that truly touched my heart. I had felt isolated and alone for so many years, and being able to have a real conversation with someone about my hopes, dreams, failures, fears, and current emotional struggles was truly invaluable.

At that time of my life, The Captain became my closest friend and the best distraction from everything else I felt was going wrong. As a working musician and performer, he seemed larger than life at times. There were always places to go and people to meet, and his wonderful sense of humor reminded me not to take life so seriously. As a friend and companion, however, Brian was kind, compassionate, and surprisingly reflective about life and the conflicts he faced as a divorced father and someone that had struggled his entire life with bouts of depression. It was probably the worst time, and the best time, to meet such an important life companion. We were both trying to come to terms with our individual situations, as well as figure out where this journey was going to take us. We were also working on becoming less broken, feeling less alienated, trying to become more connected, and reclaiming ownership of our own stories once again for good. It was kind of an intense time, but I do believe that chaos often results in some of the best creations.

The idea to start podcasting came out of the blue one night. It was blurted out on a car ride with great enthusiasm. Brian talked about his love of *The Nerdist Podcast* and his desire to just go out and talk with people. He specifically wanted to talk about people interested in Sci-Fi and so-called geek culture. I had to admit that I had never heard a podcast, but I fully supported him doing whatever it was he wanted to do. Honestly, he could have said he was going to raise unicorns on Mars at that point, and I would have told him it was a great idea. It was the first time I had seen him light up in a while, and his enthusiasm is contagious. I remember he wanted me to listen to a podcast, so I would know what he was going to be doing. He put on an episode of *The Nerdist Podcast with Chris Hardwick*. I have never been a celebrity worshipper, and the notion of listening to a famous person getting interviewed didn't appeal to me that much. I did, however, give it a chance. The conversation started slowly for me. To this day, I have to shamefully admit that I can't even remember the name of the guest that was being interviewed, and perhaps my memory is foggy on if it even was *The Nerdist Podcast*. I know that's a horrible thing for a podcaster to admit, but it's my truth. What did stick out to me in that podcast, though, was a conversation the interviewer and interviewee were having about death, and remembering someone after they are gone. The gist of the conversation was that as long as we talk about our ancestors by name after they are gone, they are always truly alive. That was something I could relate to as I thought about my grandparents and the people that had left me before I was ready to say goodbye. At that moment, I felt a connection with these strangers, and I wanted to hear more. At that moment, I realized that podcasting was storytelling.

As Brian took to the streets searching for guests and began recording his very first episodes of *The Captain's Pod*, I eagerly listened to his podcasts each week for those points in the conversation when I could truly connect to the people he was interviewing and hear their personal narratives. Listening in my car on the way home from work, I'd often find myself laughing and sometimes crying as people shared snippets of their personal lives. I fell in love with the people and their stories more so than that specific topic they were slotted to talk about.

As time went on, it became obvious that Brian was also looking for that same level of raw honesty and authentic narrative in each of *The Captain's Pod* episodes. He didn't want to just record something to say he was recording. He truly wanted to produce something that helped people feel more connected and less alien. This made it more challenging for him to decide on weekly topics and find people to interview. He grew increasingly harder on himself with every episode. A bit of that old self-doubt started working its way back into his thinking, and I was extremely worried that he didn't recognize how enjoyable the podcast was to listen to and what a positive part of his life this had become.

One May evening in 2015, Brian was over at my apartment all out of sorts because he had not interviewed a guest for the podcast that was supposed to be released the following day. He had recorded 24 *Captain's Pod* episodes at this point, and he was proud of himself for having been able to maintain the momentum of releasing an episode a week. This was going to be the first time since he started podcasting that he didn't have a show to release. I could see the despair set in, and I tried brainstorming with him possible people to interview on the spot. It just seemed like every potential suggestion was a dead end. I racked my brain for a possible solution. All I could think of was that I had been reading this book called *The Highly Sensitive Person* by Dr. Elaine Aron, and I had wanted Brian to take a questionnaire that measured sensitivity for quite a while. So much had been going on with work and the podcast, however, that we hadn't had any time to sit down and talk about it. As more of a joke than an actual idea, I said under my breath that we should talk about this book, and he should record us taking this questionnaire.

There was a very long pause, followed by him sitting straight up from the spot he had been laying in on my living room floor. Knowing my more reserved nature, he questioned if I was serious. I think I replied with a maybe, but that was enough for Brian to turn into The Captain and start plotting out the logistics of the episode. I don't remember any of the technical aspects that went into recording episode #25 of *The Captain's* Pod HSP- Highly Sensitive Persons: The Captain Gets Interviewed. I am a quiet, introverted teacher. I am far removed from the world of entertainment, and I suffer from debilitating anxiety at times with performance anxiety topping the list. Brian's enthusiasm, mixed with my exuberance for talking about a book and topic I am truly passionate about, propelled the interview. I ignored the microphone, cables, and contraptions and just focused on the conversation with Brian. I had always suspected that the outwardly comical character of The Captain was just a makeshift shield for the softer side of Brian that needed protection. He reminded me so much of the other men I was reading about in Dr. Elaine Aron's book, that I felt like it was a disservice not to clue him in, and to do for him what he was doing for others. I essentially wanted him to see that he wasn't broken or an anomaly. He was not alone.

After the recording and airing of *The Captain's Pod #25*, Brian told me that I needed to do my own show. He said that there are people out there like me that needed to hear what I had to say, and that's how *HSP SOS: Highly Sensitive Persons Saving Our Sensitivity* came about. I've spent a lot of my life listening to and observing others. I've struggled with childhood trauma, severe anxiety, and far too much self-doubt in my life. Not only has recording podcasts helped me to realize I have a voice, but it had also helped me to recognize that I can use my voice to connect with and help other people.

It has been humbling to see how many other people out there can relate to topics we discuss on *The Captain's Pod, HSP SOS,* and *In/ Ex Adventures.* People from all over the world send us messages to share their thoughts on high sensitivity, personality traits, anxiety, depression, introvert/ extrovert relationships, as well as other topics we discuss on our podcasts. It's mind-blowing at times, but it's also an affirmation that you don't have to be a "somebody" to have something to say. You just have to be yourself. Podcasting allows us all to have those intimate conversations we so desperately need in an increasingly digitally disconnected world. Thanks to Brian "The Captain" Kovacs and the magic of podcasting I truly do feel like I have a voice for the first time in my life, and I am free to be myself.

Michelle Lynn has appeared as a host on *HSP SOS*

Molly Southgate

My name is Molly Southgate and podcasting has been a part of my life since I was 6 ½. My wonderful parents, Rob and Martha Southgate, created our network, Southgate Media Group and being the extrovert I am I decided I wanted in on the action. I love watching T.V. and I am extremely long-winded so it seemed like a perfect fit for my interests. I am homeschooled and since both of my parents work from home we have plenty of time to watch and record.

Now, at twelve years old I have guested or hosted over 500 podcast episodes, and probably have listened to double that number. My current podcast is *Read Between The Lines: A Book Podcast*. I am a food blogger and my blog *@WhatsMollyMakin'?* I am a proud contributor to NaNoWriMo and wrote my first novel through the amazing service last year, and I am also a professional actress.

But, I suppose we should start at the beginning. So, let's time travel and go back to five-year-old Molly.

I had a lot of friends when I was younger, I still have quite a few friends, but when I was little, none of them "got" me. I had to sneak my interests in through the back door. When playing make-believe, I would suggest pretty names for my friends, like River Song and Primrose. I was always Amy Pond or Katniss. Playing like this helped me to gently slip in my obsessions but it was still difficult to have your friends all be into things like Barbies and La La Loopsies while you were into things like *Doctor Who* and *Harry Potter*.

However, it all changed for me the day my parents took me to my first comic con. As we walked into Mighty Con, my mom turned to me and said, "You are about to meet your people." Nothing truer has ever been spoken. Walking through those doors was like an exclamation of geekdom. Like I was saying: "Hi! My name is Molly! Yes, I'm five-years-old, and yes, I love the same things you do, adults!" I was surrounded by a room filled with geeks, fan art, cosplay, and comic books. I went from booth to booth talking to people who understood me. They were equally passionate about books, movies, and TV shows. I was dressed as Hermione Granger and didn't have to explain who I was cosplaying or what cosplaying is. I had found my people.

My next comic con was much larger, I felt lost until I spotted artists from Mighty Con, I was so happy I shouted, "My people are here!" The friendships I've made since that first Mighty Con have fed my passions, improved my art in all of its many forms, and blessed my life in so many ways.

I learned to spot friends better after that, friends who got me. I still have most of the friends I had when I was little and as they've gotten older they've understood my obsessions and played along. I like to refer to it as "growing into geekiness." Many have even introduced me to new fandoms. Some of these fandoms I LOVE and some I don't.

I was six years old when my parents decided to start the podcast network. I love to talk so you can imagine how thrilled I was when they said that I could be a part of it. My first show was *Ever After: a Once Upon a Time Podcast*. I ran downstairs one day and enthusiastically asked to create a podcast about *Once Upon a Time*, a fantasy show about fairytale characters living in modern times. None of us had seen an episode. That didn't deter me though, I assured my parents that I could handle hosting a show and that even though the series was already three seasons in we could easily catch up by that fall. My parents said yes and it sent the three of us on quite a journey.

When I first got into *Doctor Who*, one of my biggest obsessions, I was five years old. My dad was watching it, and as I was walking through the room, the television caught my eye. I just stood there transfixed. A world I never imagined could exist, did: talking cat people, a time machine shaped like a police box, sonic screwdrivers, spunky companions, and, of course, a madman in a box. I stood there for a bit until my dad noticed me and saw my eyes as wide as flying saucers. Soon after, I was sitting on the couch watching Matt Smith eat fish fingers and custard, and I was in love. And yes, like any sane person I had a massive crush on Matt Smith. A year later, I started a podcast called, *Coo Coo for Who*. It's a Beatles reference, as I explained to my Mom who replied with, "I get your references!"

If you hate the sound of your voice, don't assume others will hate it. When I was younger, I had a Kidzoom camera, and I used to often record myself singing, talking, and performing various shows. Every time I went back and listened to myself, I thought I sounded younger than I was and I hated hearing myself. The same thing happened when listening to my early podcasts. I am so much more comfortable now, but back then it was horrible for me to listen to my voice. I was afraid to share my gifts with the world. I was scared that it wouldn't be good, scared that I would be mocked, and absolutely terrified of what others would think. When I was younger I would lie in bed when I was supposed to be asleep and I would make up all types of songs. Very rarely would I actually write those down, and God forbid anyone wanted to listen to one of them. It took until I was 10 to be able to sing a full song that I wrote, in front of my parents. I no longer have those fears. I now understand that you need to share what you know with the world. Everyone who does podcasting or is thinking about doing podcasting needs to understand that. You need to know that the world would be worse off if everyone hid. Creativity and joy drive us and our culture. I believe that doing what you love brings that joy to life. I believe that God created us to laugh, to have fun, to create, but most importantly to love. If we all hid our talents and didn't show the world what we can do and what we love, the world would be a very sorrowful place. Feed your passion, feed your creativity, and then share it with the world.

When I was younger, I hid. From the time I was born until I turned eight, I refused to work on anything. My parents had to sneak any learning in through the back door and make it sound like a game. There was potential in me but I refused to let it out, I wanted to know everything about everything, and still do, but when asked to share that knowledge I would deny it. Everything changed though.

My mom's friend died of cancer very young. She was my biggest cheerleader and was proud of everything I did. She was a phenomenal singer and every performance she would pour her heart out. When she died, something changed in me. I realized that life was short and I didn't have all the time in the world. I realized I needed to live life to the fullest. So before performances now, my Mom will look at me and say "Cammi the hell out of it."

And that's what I'm asking you all to do. Before you do anything, podcasting, acting, writing, cooking- whatever feeds your passion. I am asking you to "Cammi the hell out of it." Think- who do you know in your life that puts their all out there? Emulate them. Instead of saying Cammi, say their name, or maybe say, "live the hell out of it," or, "act the hell out of it." Do whatever floats your boat. Just remember to live boldly.

There are many ways I feed my creativity from day to day. One of the ways is through my acting. Every time I'm in a theater or rehearsal space I have a "perma-smile" on my face. I love getting to pretend to be other people. I love making new friends and getting dressed up in costumes. Another way is through my writing. I also feed my creativity, and my stomach, through cooking. I started a food blog called, *What's Molly Makin'* to share my love of food. As a homeschooler, I have a lot of time to pursue my passions and be creative. Whether it's podcasting, acting, writing, cooking, drawing, directing, or the thousand other things I do. Everything I do is creative and I infuse my passion everywhere. That is my call to action, I want you to do whatever you want, no fear, shame, or guilt.

I owe the moral of this chapter to Cammi.

Remember:

"Live the hell out of it."

Molly Southgate has appeared as a host on *Read Between the Lines, Ever After: The Once Upon a Time Podcast, Coo Coo for Who, Otherworld Theatre Presents: Gateways, Live at the Blue Box, Maybe Not the Worst Podcast Ever,* and *Ever After in Wonderland*

Olivia Richards

I have a mild obsession with television and film. Anyone who knows me can totally verify that fact. Recently, my mom told me that when I was around three years old, I would ask her to "refill" (meaning "rewind") whatever movie I had literally just finished. This wasn't an isolated incident and, to be honest, not much has changed.

I discovered my love for reviewing TV shows during my sophomore year of college. I was studying communications media (for which I now have my degree), and I wanted to take my fascination and obsession with TV one step further. This started when I began writing guest reviews for a website that my friend had recommended. I discovered my voice as a writer and was promoted to staff writer about two months later.

My introduction to podcasting happened through my coverage of a magnificent disaster of a show called *Under the Dome*. Writing for the show was amazing, but it was very much a solitary activity. I discovered a vibrant, creative community when I began live-tweeting each episode. It was such an electric feeling when each episode would begin, and I would see the flood of responses from people who were reacting their own way to the exact same thing that I was seeing.

When I was asked to be a guest on the first podcast I had ever recorded, I was extremely nervous. Writing was one thing, but recording my thoughts in live time was COMPLETELY different. When I write, I'm extremely meticulous and I tend to over-think almost every single word that appears on the page. Having a recorded conversation would mean that I could run the risk of saying something stupid, or of stammering through my thoughts. What if I talked too much, or what if I didn't talk enough? My perfectionism can be an asset, but not in this case.

This was the biggest struggle that I had to overcome as a podcaster. I thought that the more prepared and precise I was, the better I would sound on each recording. This just added to my stress and took away the excitement I felt when it was time to sit down and record. I was so caught up in my own head that I was missing the fun of just being in the moment and having a conversation with people who were equally funny, creative, and passionate. Thankfully, I grew more comfortable and relaxed with practice and time.

Unfortunately, the one insecurity I wasn't quite able to work through was the sound of my own voice. It's kind of hard to stay in the moment when I'm silently criticizing my voice every single time I open my mouth to speak. This is an insecurity that several other female podcasters have openly struggled with, and it makes me feel so much better to know that I'm not alone.

I once read a review of the podcast I was co-hosting at the time. The reviewer wrote, "Love the show, but I wish she wouldn't say 'like' and 'kind of' so much!" This particular comment stuck with me for a good while. I noticed the review was written by a man. At that moment, the realization clicked in a way that I wish it hadn't. My co-host was male, and the review wasn't targeting the content of our podcast. It was specifically criticizing how I spoke. That definitely took the wind out of my sails for a little while.

Ultimately, however, I'm glad that this happened. My biggest fear when I first started was putting myself out there and opening myself up to criticism, whether it was personal or public. That comment was my fear come to life. I saw it, it stuck with me, and I felt bad for a while. Ultimately, however, I kept going. If that comment was the absolute worst thing that could happen, then so what? This was my show, my time that I was investing, and my voice. If other people didn't like it (myself sometimes included), then they could, like, kind of get over it.

There have been plenty of amazing moments I've had as a podcaster. During my senior year of college, I received the offer to co-host a weekly podcast called *TVBinges Pilot Roundtable*. Each week during pilot season, my co-host and I would sit down after each episode to weigh in. Some pilots were incredible (looking at you, *Crazy Ex-Girlfriend*!), some were pretty forgettable, and some were so bad that the recordings would just turn into borderline therapy sessions (DEFINITELY looking at you, *Manhattan Love Story*).

This opportunity happened during one of the most stressful, uncertain times of my life. I was preparing to graduate, and everything I'd been building for the last four years was about to dramatically change. My life was internship applications, resume edits, career-building courses, and counting down the days until graduation day. To put it simply, I was a complete anxious wreck most of the time. Podcasting wasn't just a hobby, or even a resume builder for me during this time. It was a breath of fresh air when it often felt like I was drowning. Even if it was just a half-hour or 45 minutes out of my day, it was time that I wasn't editing cover letters or sending out applications. Sitting down and recording was when I felt calm and in control.

Beyond that, podcasting helped me maintain my sense of self. I was a young adult trying to transition from student to a working professional for the first time. During this time, it can be very easy to forget that you're a unique, talented person who has interesting and entirely valid thoughts and feelings. Having a creative outlet was my lifeline. When I was writing and recording, I wasn't just another name on an application, or a number printed on a page. It was my time, effort, and unique voice that I had worked so hard to develop. I was once again that little girl who couldn't wait to "refill" her favorite movies and shows. I was completely myself.

I'm not sure what my future as a podcaster will hold, but I know how proud I am of the work I've done, and how proud I am to have worked with some of the incredible people I've met along the way. Although I'm no longer active as a podcaster, I know that my work in the community has greatly influenced who I am today. I'm currently working as the social media content developer for an independent jewelry store, and I absolutely love my job. I realize that my creative identity is a huge part of what keeps me inspired and motivated in life.

My love of TV and movies is still very much alive and well. Honestly, it has probably grown even stronger at this point, if that's even possible. Maybe one day I'll even sit down with my laptop and hit the record button again! Whatever the case may be, just know that when you hear me speak or read my writing, you're listening to that little girl who simply didn't want her favorite stories to end.

My biggest piece of advice for aspiring podcasters is this: just go for it. You might feel awkward and unsure at first, but just keep practicing. Don't let your fears or insecurities stop you. Keep talking about your passions and interests, and you'll find your voice along the way. Your creative journey will help you learn so much about yourself. You'll also more than likely find an entire community of friends who share those same passions and interests. Now, keep calm and podcast on!

Olivia Richards has appeared as a host on *TVBinges Pilot Roundtable Podcast* and *Chester's Mill Report*

———

Phil Perich

It seems strange to me that most of my family and friends think of me as a podcaster and blogger these days. Four years ago I barely knew what a podcast was when I went searching for my first one to listen to. I was almost sure that a podcast was a downloadable audio recording about different topics, including TV shows, which was what I was looking for. The very first show I listened to had a host who went by the name of Lilith Hellfire. I followed her podcast on Twitter and eventually emailed her when I saw that she needed someone to talk about the *Arrow* TV show I was a fan of. I remember being so nervous as the day came around where I would talk with this complete stranger. Seeing as I knew nothing about the inner workings of podcasting, as far as I knew this woman would be broadcasting from some huge, expensive recording studio. Only later when I would begin podcasting myself, would I realize that most podcasters record from the comfort of their homes. Like many people I've had the pleasure of speaking to and working with while podcasting, I caught "the bug." I was addicted right away. After guest hosting with Lilith Hellfire a second time, she pointed me to another podcaster named Zachary Hare who was looking for a cohost for a new podcast about *The Flash* TV show. After an initial conversation with Zach, we started planning our podcast. I remember the excitement I felt; I was about to share my thoughts about my interest and hobby with the world, something I had never imagined I would be able to do before then.

For the Better

Those who know me through podcasting may find this hard to believe, but for most of my life, I have been incredibly shy. It was hard, sometimes it still is, to start a conversation with anyone who I haven't known for years. Not only has podcasting given me an outlet, a "voice" to the world, but it has also helped me evolve into a more social person. Before podcasting, just asking for help in a department store or making chit chat with a stranger in line seemed like an impossible, scary thing. But now after a few years of podcasting, I find myself opening up more to friends and family, just about anyone I may encounter during the day. So I believe I can literally say that podcasting has made me a better person, a better husband, and a better father than I would have been without the experience.

Flash of Inspiration

After Lilith herself, I believe the person who has had the greatest influence on my creative endeavors is Rob Southgate. I remember the first contact I had with Rob. When planning the *Flash* podcast with Zach, Zach had neglected to fill in a few details at first. Such as that we would be a part of the Southgate Media Group and that Rob Southgate himself was looped in on our group chats. Every time this "new guy," this stranger would interject on every decision we made from a logo, a name for our podcast, and if we could squeeze in reviews for *The Flash* and *Arrow* now.

I remember thinking, who is this nosey busybody that has a say in every little decision. I think I eventually decided to check out his Facebook profile and put two and two together when I discovered his last name. A huge sense of relief flooded through me when I realized I hadn't said anything stupid before then like "What business is it of yours?" Besides his expert advice in the fields of podcasting and entertainment, his patience with the many questions I bombard him with on a weekly, if not daily basis, I also believe Rob inspires me and everyone he comes in contact with, especially those of us on the Southgate Media Group. From his generous nature and his strong work ethic editing most of the network's podcasts, I can safely say that any success I may have in the fields of podcasting and blogging would not be possible without my time learning under Rob's tutelage.

Agents of the Bat

Next, my journey would take me into even scarier waters. Before the *Flash/Arrow Power Hour* had started with Zach, Rob had already offered me my own podcast that I could create from the ground up to cover the upcoming *Gotham* TV show and anything else Batman. After the initial swell of pride that Rob had shown this much faith in me already had worn off, then the panic set in. How would I proceed? It was another podcast based on a TV show, but there was also plenty of room for personal touches. I had just arrived in podcasting land five minutes ago. Where was I going to find a co-host to work with? Would we even get along or have chemistry? After a few awkward episodes on my own, Rob had found a co-host who wanted to talk about my topic. While I have never met Kelly Dimarzio (now Fitzgerald) in person, I found her charming and easy to talk to right away. And her love of puns sealed the deal within the first few minutes of our first talk. The podcast would have been fine right there with just the two of us, but around the same time Kelly was reaching out to Rob, I got a message through the podcast's Facebook page that would change my life for the better once again. I am an only child so I have no point of reference for this next statement, but I consider the man who would join Kelly and me on the *Before the Bat* podcast like a brother. Tyler Patrick shared my love of all things DC Comics and other popular fiction. Even my mother who has never met Tyler but only listened to a few of my podcasts says she thinks Tyler and I were separated at birth. Tyler is full of even more creative ideas than I am, it all seems to come so easy to him.

The Professor

The last (but not least) regular co-host I would meet and sync with is the man known to all fans of *The 'Nuff Said Podcast* as Charlie "The Professor" Esser. While Lilith and Tyler would be my biggest supporters and allies on the DC Comics side of podcasting, Charlie Esser was a Marvel man through and through. I figured as a regular reader of Marvel comics for close to thirty years, not many people would match my almost obsessive knowledge of Marvel Comics. Charlie Esser would prove to be my match. "The Professor" not only had a vast knowledge of how the Marvel Universe worked but was very knowledgeable about the real world as well (as one would expect from a former *Who Wants to Be a Millionaire* contestant). While some people take a while to form a partnership and/or friendship, Charlie Esser and I quickly bonded over the exploits of these fictional super people along with our desire to share our knowledge and opinions with the world. I believe all of our podcast endeavors together are so much the better due to Charlie and I challenging each other's notions of what is possible in this impossible fictional world. What If?

Speedy

Not to retread what I've already gone over, but aside from Rob Southgate, I wouldn't be where I am creatively today if it wasn't for Lilith Hellfire. After those first two episodes, Lilith and I wouldn't work together except for a few times here and there. Eventually, I asked her if she would lend her brilliance to *World's Finest*, my DC Comics review podcast. This podcast along with *Legends of DC*, which is what the *Flash/Arrow Power Hour* would evolve into would not be what they are today without her help and insights. We also do the *Queen Consolidated* podcast where we review the *Arrow* TV show, which also brings our journey full circle. My nickname for Lilith is "Speedy," after the hero's sister/sidekick. What Lilith doesn't know (until now) is that it also has a double meaning for me. I also call her this because she thinks much faster and in ways others do not, including me sometimes.

Back to the Future

And you may be asking now, where does that leave me podcasting "career" now? As I write this, Lilith, Tyler, Charlie and I are planning our own podcast named *Capes and Lunatics*. With age, hopefully, comes something close to wisdom. Instead of doing multiple podcasts with all one or two of my friends at a time, we've decided to create one place where we can focus all our energies on our "art" and hopefully create our own brand that will find fans. I know as you read this, others and I will be having fun on our new podcast because I always have a great time with these people and feel such a sense of accomplishment when I am done for the day. This chapter is dedicated to all of you I mentioned above who help me refine my craft and most importantly to my wife Danielle and son Luca, whose love and support give me strength whenever I doubt myself. And to you reading this right now, hopefully, I've inspired you to do something that will fulfill you, satisfy a creative urge, or create the world's next great masterpiece.

Phil Perich has appeared as host on *Capes and Lunatics Podcast, Capes and Lunatics Sidekicks Podcast, Before the Bat: The Gotham Podcast, Flash/Arrow Podcast, This Week in Geek, Superconnectivity, Ultimate Spidercast, Legends of the Arrowverse, Wade's World: The Deadpool Podcast, Comic Capers, Quantum Zone, Nightwing News, Angel Chronicles, World's Finest,* and *All New Marvel Roundup*

Samuel Gronseth II

Games as Lit. 101 started, believe it or not, as a high school class.

My love of video games as a storytelling medium began fairly early when my love of books led me to recognize the narrative elements in the games I was playing. Of course, college programs on the subject are rare even at the time of writing, so I majored in English and brought video games into my studies on literature and writing whenever I could. That focus culminated in a senior project developing a literature class that used video games rather than books, with an emphasis on how games specifically told stories through the player's interaction. Once I graduated I had the opportunity to teach that class at a few local schools, and discovered my love of teaching.

This class formed the foundations of *Games as Lit. 101* and creating it was one of the more interesting challenges I've faced in this whole process. Surprisingly, I found myself longing for those thick compilation books from college literature classes, the ones that would gather a variety of notable short stories and novellas into a single tome for easy access. I hated them in college, but I suddenly missed them when I was left to somehow gather a variety of video games and ensure that students would have the means to play them.

But possibly the most important thing I learned is just how much of a perspective shift is needed for most people to grasp the concept of video games as a narrative art form. I had multiple parents ask if the course was "legitimate," and if I would be making their children play *Grand Theft Auto* (as though M-rated games would be allowed in a high school course to begin with). Well-meaning teachers would regularly compliment me on how my class made their students more interested in "real literature." And even my students took months to realize that my detailed essay prompts on character development and narrative delivery didn't just mean, "Write a review about how fun this game was to play."

We live in a society that has taught us to approach video games with little to no intellectual investment, and the results of that mindset were evident as my students struggled to adjust their thinking on this medium. But over time, they did, and each essay showed a deeper and deeper understanding of both storytelling as an art form and video games as a medium for it. Seeing that improvement, knowing it was because of my guidance, was one of the most fulfilling experiences of my life.

I wish I had discovered that earlier, however, as I hadn't gone to school for teaching and couldn't turn it into a full-time job without the proper credentials. So when a better job opportunity presented itself, my wife and I moved away, and that chapter in our lives came to a close. In its absence, I adapted the ideas from the course into a web-series and began work on *Games as Lit. 101*.

My inspirations ranged from the videos of *Channel Awesome* to the educational tone of *Extra Credits* to the long-form analysis of YouTube shows like *Errant Signal* and *Brows Held High*. I wanted to try and present something casual enough to appeal to the average gamer, but ideally with enough presentation quality and depth of content to appeal to people who had never played a game in their life.

I'm never quite sure how well I've struck that balance, but I suppose the show's growing fan-base suggests I'm not too far off the mark.

At first, the biggest challenge was sticking with it; the show was slow to grow at first, but these things wither and die if they don't get regular attention, so I kept going. Over time the show grew, I began forming a relationship with my viewer base, and it became a very affirming experience.

It's not experience without its mistakes, of course. My first episode (a narrative analysis of *Prince of Persia: The Sands of Time*) was filmed before I got an onboard mic, and the result is such terrible audio that I'm still considering redoing the video entirely. A later plan to analyze the entire *Gears of War* trilogy in one video became a quadrilogy of videos investigating the series' aspirations and thematic shortcomings. And I still get comments on my *Bioshock* video about my mistaken statement that the philosophy of objectivism considers charity to be immoral. Doing these sorts of things is always a learning experience.

When starting the show, I put a bit of money into some simple equipment to improve the show's presentation (mainly professional lighting, a decent camera, and an onboard mic), and I would definitely recommend aspiring YouTubers to do the same. It's hard to make a name for oneself on YouTube, and there are already plenty of people talking about stuff on their webcams; a bit of production quality early on goes a long way toward making a show stand out. When you invest enough in your equipment to make you look more professional, potential viewers will more easily believe you have something worthwhile to say.

It's also important to be visible and available and reach out to other people doing similar work. The easiest tool for this in my experience is Twitter since it's relatively easy to make contact with people and get noticed by them; that's how I became involved with the *Gaming Symposium* podcast (which features three other YouTubers who host similar shows). Being generally available to people helps build rapport with your viewer base and increases your visibility, allowing for more opportunities as your show grows.

Games as Lit. 101 most consistently surprises me, though, with which videos gain the most popularity. Sometimes it's fairly predictable; I'm not at all surprised that *Bioshock* is my most watched analysis, for instance. But I still don't know why my *Little Inferno* analysis led to one of my biggest subscriber boosts to this day, or why an episode coinciding with the release of a major movie got so little attention.

The show has definitely become a major staple of my life. *Games as Lit. 101* has afforded me some exciting opportunities, put me in a position to connect with other gaming critics I respect a good deal, and most importantly, it serves as a good outlet for me to express my ideas about video games as they grow into an increasingly refined and culturally relevant art form.

I'm hoping to eventually do the show full-time (something that, at the time of writing, my wife and I are working to make a reality) because I truly believe if I had the time and energy to put into it the channel could stand a real chance at success. But it's surprising how difficult it can be to focus on such things with a full-time job that bears no relation to it. Whereas inspiration would regularly strike and I'd have a new episode written out within an hour, I now sit down and struggle for hours to write a workable script, let alone a good one. This drain on my emotional and creative energy has negatively affected the show for the last year or two. This is the show's greatest difficulty at the moment, and I'm hoping for the opportunity to give the show the attention it deserves and, hopefully, gain the support necessary to continue doing so.

But when I do get a video out, I remember why I do this. Why I love it so much. Not just because I love video games, or enjoy the process of digging deeper into their narrative mechanisms, but because both video games and the people who play them need more voices doing just that. I'm not the loudest of these voices, and I'm certainly not the best, but I'm still making an impact. That's all I want from this.

Ultimately, I do the show because I want to contribute however I can to the growing rhetoric around video games as an art form and a storytelling medium, but what truly keeps me going is the response from people who understand or appreciate a game more because of my videos. There's still part of me that wants to be a teacher, I suppose, and the pride of knowing people are better off for my work is a powerful reward.

Samuel Gronseth II has appeared as host on *Games as Lit. 101, The Gaming Symposium,* and *Level Story Magazine*

Scott L. Clark

I got into podcasting for the same reason I assume most of us did. I had been listening to shows for years and thought to myself, "I can do that." Listening to other shows truly inspired me to branch out on my own while giving me an outlet to discuss my favorite hobby. I wanted a place where I could gush about what I loved without judgment by people who actually shared my enthusiasm. The Internet seemed like the most likely (albeit dangerous) place to make that happen. Podcasting became almost a natural step for me in that pursuit.

My first step into producing my own show was definitely a learning experience. I had no clue what I was doing. My first show was called *The Official Thread Podcast*. We literally recorded our pilot episode in a closet. I'll never forget sitting at the card table, hanging clothes on one side of me, and my good friend, Chris Owens, on the other. Mike Card, my other co-host at the time, was on the other end of the country talking with the two of us over Skype. Our sound quality was terrible. We had a very loose format. Not a single one of us was very good in front of the microphone. But boy, did we have a great time discussing video games. It was a great feeling to be having a conversation with friends like I always did, but this time there was one big difference: purpose. We may have been shooting the breeze like we always had in the past, but now we had a potential audience, and that was one of the greatest feelings in the world.

Sadly, *The Official Thread* didn't last very long. Being new to podcasting took its toll on my numbers, and I became very discouraged very quickly. My attention quickly turned to my second podcast, *The Hollywood Outsider,* which focused on movies and television shows. This was the brainchild of my close friend, Aaron Peterson, who had a web site by the same name when I had initially met him ten years prior. The podcast became a natural extension of what he had already established so many years ago, and he took a more fastidious approach to sound quality, formatting, and marketing. I owe the majority of my podcasting expertise to Aaron and his determination to only be satisfied with the very best overall experience for our listeners. After six years, The HO is still going strong, and I've made countless friends, industry contacts, and had incredible experiences over the years.

As much as I love movies and television, my passion has always been video games. Four years after co-founding *The Hollywood Outsider*, I decided to, once again, try my hand at another show focused on my favorite hobby. I resolved to do things differently this time around and learn from the mistakes I made with *The Official Thread*, and from the successes, Aaron taught me with *The Hollywood Outsider*.

My first step was my decision to make a podcast that I would want to hear if I were on the other end of an episode. I had grown tired of so many video game journalists who had fallen into a niche of negativity when it came to talking about games. It was very easy for podcasters to heavily criticize other people's art and focus on what didn't work for them. One podcaster gave me hope that it was, indeed, possible to be positive and entertaining at the same time. I began listening to Jeff Cannata (jeffcannata.com) when he became a regular on a show called *Weekend Confirmed,* which was hosted by Garnett Lee. Jeff was a beacon of positive light in an industry that seems so focused on being negative. He gushed about the games he loved while still being critically fair and honest about glaring issues. Jeff never relished in bashing or tearing down games for being awful; in fact, his tone was one of genuine constructive criticism. But once he got on a roll about a game he loved, I adored sitting back and soaking up his enjoyment in a way that reminded me why I enjoyed playing video games in the first place. Jeff developed a reputation: he "loves loving things." It made me sad that many considered this a bad thing, especially since I idolized him so much for it. I still listen to Jeff to this day on his shows "DLC" and "We Have Concerns."

I finally decided to give a gaming podcast another shot. After much deliberation with a couple of friends from a video game forum on Rotten Tomatoes, *The Gaming Outsider* was born. Josh Faulkner, Zach Anderson, and I had been interacting online with one another for well over fifteen years. All were passionate and knowledgeable about games and agreed to a weekly commitment to record a show. I explained to both of them my goal for the show: one that focused on what we enjoyed about gaming while still being critics toward the games we played. We wanted no part in any political arguments, and we wanted a light-hearted tone with hosts that didn't necessarily have to agree with one another all the time. To this day, we end every episode with our sign-off: "There's no such thing as a bad game, just games that aren't for you." While we don't say this mantra in the literal sense, we've accepted that what might not have been a great experience for us, could be someone else's favorite. This mentality has given us an air of respect for each other, our listeners, and our community.

My biggest roadblock was finding that one thing that set me apart from other similar podcasts. I decided to take an approach that would kill two birds with one stone by offering something to listeners that most podcasts don't while also acting as a way to spread the word about *The Gaming*

Outsider. Josh, Zach, and I host the show each week, but we also offer a rotating fourth chair to any listener or podcaster that is willing to sit and talk video games with us for a couple of hours. In this way, the listeners truly feel like a part of the show. On top of that, they're more likely to share the podcast with their friends and families. This serves as a natural marketing tool for us and also allows me to offer something to other podcasters who are looking to cross-promote. We've had a lot of success with this strategy, and I love meeting so many new people who are just as passionate about games as I am.

If I had to give a new podcaster any advice, it would be these three things. First, be prepared to work hard and accept the fact that you might fail. If you do fail, as I did, be ready to pick yourself up and try again after you've figured out where you went wrong. As long as you learn from your mistakes, it's completely fine to make them. Secondly, find yourself a dedicated team that is willing to put forth as much effort as you. Unless you're doing it full-time, it's difficult to do all of the prep work, recording, editing, and posting all by yourself. You'll want to delegate the responsibilities to keep what's supposed to be a fun hobby from feeling like work. Finally, find a way to market yourself by offering something to new listeners. I'm not saying you should have an open seat on your show like we do, but cross-promoting is much easier when you have that "give first" mentality going into it. Most others in the industry are probably just as eager to get the word out about their work as you are, so offer to promote them first and ask them to reciprocate.

OK, one more piece of advice: have fun podcasting. If it stops being fun, your listeners will hear it in your voice, and your show will instantly become less interesting. Do whatever you can to keep each episode fresh, exciting, topical, and fun to listen to. If you don't, neither you nor your listeners will have an enjoyable experience. And if that's not happening, then what's the point?

Scott L. Clark has appeared as host on *The Official Thread Podcast, The Hollywood Outsider, The Gaming Outsider,* and *Packers Fan Podcast*

Scott Ryder

I believe it was sometime in 2011 that my friends and I began talking about starting a podcast. At the time, my brother Brian was on a weekly podcast with his friend Nicole. I do not remember the name of the show, but it was on Blog Talk Radio live every week. I remember listening to their show and thinking that, since I went to college partially for Audio Engineering, I could produce a way better show, as they were all sitting in her basement with a microphone hanging from the ceiling.

Soon after that that Nicole offered us a show on her account. From there, Brian, Matt, Joe, Ken and I started the *Who Are The Area Men* show. This was our Sunday morning live show where we basically talked about current events, television, and movies. The idea was that each person would bring at least one thing to talk about and hopefully that would spark discussions to fill the two-hour time slot. This only lasted a few months.

It wasn't long before the show began falling apart. As you can imagine, five people on one live show can be a nightmare. While Brian was the official "host" of the show, everyone else always wanted to be the star. On top of that, Brian and I were mostly on the same page, but Ken and Matt had their own ideas on what they wanted the show to be. Brian and I wanted to keep it light and fun, while Ken wanted to do more serious topics to start arguments because his friends liked to hear him and Brian argue. While Matt, admittedly, had the weekly goal of derailing the show.

This really brought out the tensions to the point where Brian did not want to host anymore, and everyone else loved to point that out in order to start fights on the air. I ran the controls, so to speak, on Blog Talk Radio so one particular Sunday, as everyone was bickering, I decided that if nobody had anything constructive to say, I was just going to end the show, which I did. Effectively putting the last nail in the coffin for *Who Are The Area Men*.

After everyone had time to cool down, we all started to reminisce about the good times we had podcasting. Since Brian, Joe and I had more free time than anyone else, we decided to test the waters. This time, I opened my own account through Podbean, started recording/editing the shows, and we were on our way again. July 22th, 2014, the very first *Comic Roast* podcast took the Internet by storm. Well, not really, but the three of us started podcasting regularly again.

This lasted for about a month before Ken decided he missed podcasting as well. Since he was not into comics as heavily as the rest of us, and we learned our lesson with too many people, we started a second show. Brian, Ken and I became *The Night Beard Show*. This show was more like what we were doing with *Who Are The Area Men*, only now that it was being edited, and was much better.

Once again, a few more weeks go by, and Nicole wants to be a part of what we are doing. Enter the *You Talk Too Much Podcast*. Our third weekly podcast where we discussed whatever topic that Nicole brought to the table. Probably our most interesting podcast, but sadly it did not last very long. Although, this was when we decided that maybe we should start our own podcast network. So, taking from our first podcast (Area Men), we started the AMP Network (Area Men Podcasting Network).

Things seemed to be going great for us this time

around. Our shows were way better than they ever were and we were all much happier as well. We started a lot of cross promoting with other shows. We increased our social media presence, and we were always on the lookout for people to come podcast with us. While things seemed to be going so well, we started to have Chris, current *Comic Roast* member, guest host once a month or so.

Then again, things started falling apart. Joe was frequently silent for entire shows, or just sitting them out completely. While Ken started having issues with our content to the point where he didn't want to do the show if we didn't discuss his topics. At this point, Brian and I were determined to make this work no matter what. So, after sitting down with Joe and having him basically quit, we told him he was always welcome back and that we will consider it a hiatus. And as far as *The Night Beard Show*, we decided to turn it into a movie podcast. Brian, Ken and I would take turns picking a movie that at least one of us had not seen and then we would discuss/review it. Great!

It was shortly after this little hiccup that Chris started Skyping in every week, replacing Joe full time. This was also around the time that Ken decided that he did not want to talk about movies and he quit *The Night Beard Show*. Once again, Brian and I put the pieces back together so to speak and started *The Movie Roast*.

Now that we had everything back to some normalcy, our friend Mike decided to throw his hat into the ring. Enter the creation of *Review & Roast*, our review website that we run concurrent to the podcast. We began working on the site around April of 2015, and I believe we finally went live with the site June 1st, 2015. This took a lot of effort since I was still podcasting twice a week with Brian, designing a website, and writing as many reviews as possible for the launch of the website.

Now, in order to (hopefully) get off to a strong start, we took our creation to Wizard World Chicago a few months later with a booth of our very own. We ordered all kinds of promotional materials for this. We had keychain bottle openers, water bottles and coffee mugs to give away as well as seven long boxes of comics that were gifted to us. And, to draw people to our booth, we raffled off the complete New Mutants run that included the first appearance of Cable as well as the first appearance of Deadpool right as the Deadpool movie was in full hype! We were hoping to make a killing. Instead, Wizard World almost killed our spirits.

Mike was fairly disappointed in the fact that, since he paid for almost everything, that he did not make nearly what he has spent. I, on the other hand, was happy that we at least walked away with a few hundred Instagram followers and a few thousand Facebook followers. Not ideal, but better than nothing.

Since then, we have added a few more podcasts to the mix. We still have *The Comic Roast*, which is now comprised of Brian, Chris, Demian, and myself, that comes out every Monday, as well as, *You May Or May Not Like It* with Brian, Mike, and I. That one used to come out whenever we had something to talk about, but has since turned into a board game podcast we release every Thursday. We still have *Review & Roast Presents*, which is pretty much our interview podcast where our crowning achievements, in my opinion, are our interview with Bob Fingerman, creator of the comic Minimum Wage, and our interview with actor Keith Powell from *30 Rock* and his web series *Keith Broke His Leg*.

What else can I say? Overall, it can be a lot of work. Between recording, editing, scheduling podcasts, maintaining and updating the website, and reviewing as much as I can, all while holding down a regular 9 - 5, it can get overwhelming. But, I love it, and I will never give it up.

Scott Ryder has appeared as host on *The Comic Roast, The Movie Roast, Review and Roast, You May or May Not Like It, You Talk Too Much,* and *Who Are The Area Men*

Scott Troiano

I am a fraud.

Everything I do is an unmitigated lie.

Parent? I have no idea what I'm doing raising kids. Trying my hardest and failing regularly. I try to learn from my failures. I had to train more to get the license to drive my car!

Adult? I have no idea what I am doing from day to day getting through life, work, and week in - week out. I try to get it right.

Person? I have had screwed up relationships, been fired, almost been evicted, kicked out of more than one University, and wandered around for the better part of two decades before figuring out what the word 'career' meant. I have no idea what I've been doing for the majority of my life.

Podcaster? Did someone give me a mic? No, actually I bought the mic on my own and have been strangling it for the better part of 4 years now.

But to say I am an expert in any of those things above is likely a lie. I'm a fake. A Fraud. I have no idea what I am doing.

I have the double whammy of having both Narcissistic Personality Disorder (NPD) and Impostor Syndrome. In a nutshell (and in VERY layman's terms), the first is that I need constant validation and affirmation because every action I perform will ultimately never be good enough and the second is a deep-seated fear that at any moment someone in the crowd is going to point out that I am faking it all. That someone, at any moment, will jump out and yell, "AH HA!" with a finger pointed and a scowling look on their face. It is this fear that I have lived most my life. It is this fear that I started podcasting. Everything I do in the podcasting world is a lie.

It all starts with the phrase "Fake it 'till you make it." No one truly knows that you don't know what you are doing, so if you act like you do, most people will buy it. My father coined it much better when we were sitting courtside for a Pacer game. "Act like you belong here." The notion that when the waitress comes to take your order courtside that you behave as though this is normal because it is. You mark yourself as someone who does not belong when you react in amazement that such things exist. When you sit in the cheap seats, you get your own drinks.

That ability to 'Act like I belong here' was fostered in me at a very early age. The advice to fake it till you make it is used in social settings, work, and all-around life. Most prized in our societies are the 'experts.' Experts are the ones who are comfortable with where they are, with what they know, and with getting the job done. Experts demand our attention, command our respect, and are considered the oracles of Truth. Many times in my life I have faked being an Expert. Many times I have acted like I belonged in the Expert's chair. I act like I belong there. And have gotten good at faking it.

While I was born at a very young age, I started to role-play when I was 8. My father bought the *D&D* and *AD&D* books for me on my 8th birthday from the bookstore. I started playing and enjoying myself. I read nearly everything the game world had to offer. By the age of 18, I had been running games for a decade and had spent a horrible amount of disposable income on gaming materials. By the age of 28, I had been to major events, watched Gary Gygax run games, and been to nearly every major gaming convention except for GenCon. By 38 years of age, I had attended GenCon several times, had been running what would become the longest Live Action Roleplaying game ever run in Indiana, and was, somehow, an expert in running a roleplaying game. How did I become an expert? I don't know. I was faking it that whole time. How did I run a game that ran for 11 and ½ years? I just faked it for that long. Somewhere along the way, people started suggesting Scott might know the answers to the really hard questions. All the while, I was having fun, not becoming an expert. At least not in my mind.

In 2013 someone suggested that I should make a podcast. I said that I would, it sounded fun, and I like hearing the sound of my own voice. I said I would, but I dragged my feet. I didn't know anything about podcasting. I am not an authority on anything. What did I know? What was I good at? My day job is managing a group of computer developers writing software for mobile apps at a well-known bank. Nobody wants to hear about that. (Actually, I think there may be ground to cover there, but that's not been recorded yet...) But I did know about gaming. So this person said, "You should record what you know. You should tell people how to run a great game. Or at least run a game and record THAT and let people listen to how you do it." I continued to drag my feet. Was I good enough? Would people know that I was faking it? Would I be caught when one of my listeners shouted, "AH HA!" and revealed me as a fraud?

I was the guest on a roleplaying game that was hosted by another podcaster. He had me on for the better part of 4 months before I got truly comfortable. Now, from day one I was faking it. I sounded good because I acted like I belonged on the mic. I was just having more fun.

In 2014, I finally bought a mic that sat in the middle of the table that recorded everything from our voices to the lawnmower down the street. I recorded a few episodes with my friends. They were awful. I delayed my content until I had 16 weeks of material in the can. I then started to release. When I look back now, it was horrific. But it was more than anyone else I knew running a game was doing. I was on the cutting edge, and I had no idea what I was doing. But I could fake it. And it was fun.

I found a core group of players who were very good at being adults. There were one or two that came and went over the course of a year. We found an equilibrium. We had fun.

After a year, we got better equipment. Our sound was much better, very professional. It sounded fun.

After that year, one game became two became three. We were becoming good at faking this podcasting thing. We were good at having fun.

One game crumbled because of drama. We learned what not to do. We learned that we need boundaries. We need structure. We need balance. We learned how to fake those things. Our other games were protected because we wanted to continue to have fun.

We added convention coverage to our lineup. Our audience started to grow. We have been working for more than a year to strive to become the voice of Gaming/Pop Culture/Geek/Nerd conventions in central Indiana, having fun all the while. This season we were contacted by two conventions that invited us to join them to podcast their events. It was a lot of fun.

I was asked to write a chapter for this book. The notion was absurd to me. Why would anyone want to know my journey to become a podcaster? I am a fraud. Why would anyone want to read what I do or what I have to say? I have been faking it for so long that it seems to me that nothing about who I am is real. But we set up the mics...we level the sound, and then we hit record and start with, "Gooooood evening ladies and gentlemen, and welcome to Gaming with Scott, I'm here with...." And the transformation is immediate. It is substantive. It is miraculous. It's fun.

We create. We spin tails. We tell stories. We make art.

I am the expert. I am the control. I am the host of *Gaming with Scott*.

There is no fear.

There is no worry.

There is no outside world.

We are the experts.

We are the Kings and Queens and rulers of our domain.

Listeners may not agree. Heck, we have a running joke that our episodes are so bad that we get down to negative one listener.

There is no fear.

There is no doubt.

We are not acting.

We belong here.

We Podcast.

Creation is its own reward.

Creation is not a lie.

I am not a failure.

I am not a fraud.

I am part of *Gaming With Scott*.

Scott Troiano has appeared as host on *Gaming With Scott: Marvel Live Play*, *Gaming With Scott: Stargate SG10*, *Gaming With Scott: Star Trek Adventures*, *Gaming With Scott: Fantasy Weekly*, *Gaming With Scott: Behind the Masks*, *Gaming With Scott: Annual Halloween Extravaganza* and *Masks of Nyarlathotep*.

Troy Heinritz

"We have to go back, Kate. WE HAVE TO GO BACK!"

No better words can describe TV fandom in the spring of 2007. For me, it was the calling to return to my roots of the broadcasting medium I had gone to school for, but never got a job in. Podcasting was just getting its footing, but it was the TV show *LOST* that really opened the door to the concept of a global community, listening to like-minded voices through these "internet radio shows" called podcasts. I was enamored by the likes of *The Lost Cast with Jay and Jack*, *Lostcasting with Wayne and Dan*, and *The Weekly Lost Podcast* from GSPN.TV. All these people were discussing something I couldn't stop talking about. The watercooler at work was dry; no one watched the show but, yes oh yes, I found my tribe and the doors that opened afterward are an amazing story.

I didn't begin my own podcast until 2013, see when you have little ones they take up a lot of your time. But I wasn't sitting idly by. No, I was researching, listening, and understanding what it takes to be a Cliff Ravenscraft, a Wayne Henderson, a Jay and Jack. I started asking Wayne questions since he also produced a Green Bay Packers podcast as well as one for the TV show *Fringe*, both things absolutely loved.

Podcasting starts with P, the same letter used in Passion, Purpose, and People. I had a passion but what was my purpose? Who were my people? Wayne Henderson was both. Listening to Wayne over five years really let me connect with this person. Can you connect with someone you never see face to face? Apparently so, because in 2012 plans were underway to launch our first podcast together, *Under The Dome Radio*.

It's all about the name of your podcast. Include the title of the TV show. Check. Include something relatable about the content (there is a radio station in the book that is key to the storyline). Check. Find a co-host who loves the material as much as you. Check. And so UnderTheDomeRadio.com was born, and a new partnership began. But this partnership had its challenges, Wayne was on the west coast and I was on the east coast. How were we going to do a post-show podcast if Wayne didn't even see it and I was fast asleep? We pooled Wayne's existing audience members to help him get a SlingBox that we installed at my house, which allowed him to watch in real-time with me. Three seasons and 74 podcast episodes later, we escaped from *Under The Dome* wondering what do next. Passion, People, Purpose. This time we had a purpose; to keep entertaining our loyal fan base. But it took people, or in this case a person, to inspire the next part of the story. Enter Kevin Sizemore.

Kevin is an actor of a different breed, he is a Christian and when you are a Christian working in a place like Hollywood things can be challenging. So one day this young, eager podcaster reached out to him about his bible verse on his twitter account, and a friendship was born. Kevin appeared on two episodes of *Under The Dome*, but it was enough to secure an interview with him, build that bond, and solidify Wayne and Troy in his brain. The passion of our next project was to find a *LOST*-like TV show. Luckily, ABC was going to air *Resurrection* in the spring of 2014, a story of people long dead coming back to life! Bingo and we're off.

In the winter of 2013, I received a phone call from Kevin saying that he was going to be in the first season of this new show *Resurrection* on ABC and told us to podcast about it. When we told him we already had it in the works he called the powers that be at ABC. During that first season of *Resurrection*, we had the opportunity to interview series creator Aaron Zellman, author Jason Mott who penned the novel *The Returned* which was the basis for the TV show, and almost the entire cast during the first season. Again Passion, People, Purpose the three pillars to a successful podcast.

People started to take notice of our work. A few friends told us about a new Podcast network called TV Talk that was starting up where for 20-30 minutes you would talk about a TV show, send it in to a producer, and the next morning BOOM – instant morning drive podcast. I applied for a few shows that I had a passion for, but none was greater than the new TV show coming on in the fall of 2013 called *The Blacklist*. TV Talk was amazing, and we met so many cool podcasting friends like Aaron Peterson from *The Hollywood Outsider Podcast*, The Real Brian from *The Real Brian Show*, and Darrell Darnell from Golden Spiral Media among others. The first year of TV Talk: *The Blacklist* was some of the most fun because we had to talk about 44 minutes of content in 22 minutes or less and *The Blacklist* had as much mythology as a *LOST, FRINGE,* or *ALIAS* episode. Sadly the network folded after the first year but since there was still a passion (We LOVE *The Blacklist*), a purpose (We need our community to help keep this story straight), and our People – Blacklist Fandom, I knew this show needed to continue.

That's where Aaron Peterson and Darrell Darnell join the story. Although podcasting can take place anywhere around the world, I wanted to partner with someone that had similar interests and also lived close to do some collaboration and fan meetups. Aaron was only an hour or so from me, so he agreed to be the new co-host of *The Blacklist Exposed*.

Darrell being our TV Talk producer invited us to join his network and Brian our old editor gave us tips to make the show sound spectacular. Ten episodes later of the new version of our *Blacklist* podcast we were nominated as one of the top 10 Entertainment podcasts for 2015. AH-MAZING! And it was a nomination that stemmed from the fan community not a panel of industry professionals. We had something magical. We honored that magic by letting the fans take over our Season 2 Fan Feedback Finale (Episode 27 of *The Blacklist Exposed*), which caught the attention of a few people associated with the show. People once again took us the next step.

Kicking off-season 3 we had the honor to interview one of the writers for *The Blacklist*, Daniel Knauf, which to this day is one of the most profound interviews I have listened to (Episode 30 of *The Blacklist Exposed*). Shortly after that interview aired season 3 kicked off and one Jon Bokenkamp, creator of *The Blacklist* sent us a tweet asking to be on our show. Two guys in a basement, no marketing budget, is this really happening? Jon came on the show for a mid-season 3 discussion that is still the most listened to episode of the podcast to date. That sparked a domino effect opening doors to talk to actors like Amir Arison (Aram Mojtabai), Hisham Tawfiq (Dembe Zuma) and series star Megan Boone (Elizabeth Keen). We also helped promote merchandise such as the Elizabeth Keen Dossier, an in-world add on written by Paul Terry and Tara Bennet as well as a RED vinyl record featuring songs from the first season of *The Blacklist* for Record Store Day. Passion, Purpose, People what would happen next.

Enter Caroline Mendoza, Public Relations Manager for the show at Sony Television who owned the show. She recommended that with our reach into the fan-base that we should come to Los Angeles to interview Jon Bokenkamp and John Eisendrath (Executive Producer) for a season four promotional show called *Behind The Blacklist*. What an amazing opportunity to take our thoughts, the fans' thoughts, directly to the powers that be and grill them for an hour to get the answers we wanted to see in Season 4. The footage went into the promotional piece that aired internationally on channels like Sky Living (now Sky 1) in the United Kingdom, Yahoo 7 in Australia and Global TV in Canada as well as NBC here in the United States to name a few. This helped boost the podcast even more as we entered season 4. But the people were leaving and ratings were dropping; we need a new purpose. Purpose! Get people excited about *The Blacklist* again.

Dateline Chicago – April 22nd, 2017, a room of 250+ fans of *The Blacklist* gather as well as thousands online to see one Amir Arison who had one of his biggest episodes on *The Blacklist* air not just two days prior as well as Susan Blommaert who plays the enigma, Mr. Kaplan. They are accompanied by one creator Jon Bokenkamp at a fan panel for C2E2, a comic and entertainment expo in Chicago, hosted by none other than Aaron and myself from *The Blacklist Exposed Podcast*. Two days before the event, *The Blacklist* returned on NBC with its 16th and 17th episodes of the fourth season to the resounding applause from fans. *The Blacklist* is back! A two-hour cornucopia of information as an episode that fans had been asking for since season two finally made the airwaves, The Mr. Kaplan backstory. Revealing more in that hour than had been revealed in the 82 episodes prior (plus eight spinoff episodes in *The Blacklist: Redemption)*. Fans were once again reunited around the show they loved and to say thank you, a podcast brought their heroes to them live and in stereo. But the powers that be rewarded them even further. Word had gotten to us that one of our most avid fans in *Blacklist* nation was not going to be with us much longer. With her passing, we, just two guys in a basement, reached out to Jon letting him know of the situation. What happened was an amazing tribute to the fan and her family. A character in the show was named after her but not just a sideline character. No. A character that would directly help save Raymond Red Reddington's life. The one character Lou Lou loved the most.

Why do we podcast? We have a passion to make the world a better place each and every day. Opening up the microphone knowing that you can make one person's life just that much brighter is worth more than any money or swag we could receive for our efforts. We have passion. No one loves work, but we will work for what we love. Touching people through common interests brings us closer together in our humanity. That is what I want to work for. We have people, both loyalists and those who think we are off our rocker, but they are our people, our fandom, and our friends. Without them, our words would be lost to the ether. So thank you to everyone who has been on this journey with me, we have only just begun.

Troy Heinritz has appeared as host on *The Blacklist Exposed - "2017 Academy of Podcasters Award Winner" - Podcast Awards 5x Nominee, Beyond Westworld - Podcast Awards 2x Nominee, Packers Fan Podcast - Podcast Awards 5x Nominee, 11.22.63: A Look Back, Resurrection Revealed, Under The Dome Radio, Remake this Movie RIGHT! - Podcast Awards 3x Nominee, The Hollywood Outsider - (recurring guest) 2018 Podcast Awards Winner and 8x Nominee, TV Talk Revenge, and TV Talk The Blacklist*

Wendi Freeman

I host a podcast called *Double Page Spread*. I was a recording engineer for a number of years in Philadelphia. I've always worked in comic shops and had a lifelong love of comics. I remember hearing about podcasting and thinking I could combine the two things I'm into. On my podcast, I interview comic book creators. I talk to all kinds of artists and writers, and I love hearing about the artistic process and what makes people tick. The podcasts that inspired me are *11 O'Clock Comics* and John Suintres on *Word Balloon*. They are the godfathers of comic book podcasting.

I had been wrestling with the idea of how to make my show stand out. I didn't want to be just another interview show. For a while I had local comic creators coming over and cooking or eating with me. We're in the kitchen together. We're talking about stuff, but then you get all these sounds of chopping. It was a horrible idea for an audio-only podcast.

I've had so many wonderful guests on my show. One time I had John DeMatteis on. He was a writer on Spider-Man who wrote *Kraven's Last Hunt*. He's a legendary Marvel writer and is absolutely fascinating. John's a wealth of information. I had him on and we did a whole episode where we played Beatles trivia together. He's always really positive and insightful. I enjoyed that a lot.

I think it's fun to go off format. One time I had Crispin Glover on an episode and he's in no way related to comics. I like it when you could get oddball guests. You can't just presume that your listenership is only into one thing, or they're only interested in this one type of person. And you can't presume fans of your oddball guests wouldn't also get into comic book conversations.

I podcast out of curiosity and out of a compulsion - to know more about people. I like the friendships I've built. I like having people know me for something. I've made a tremendous amount of friends and real connections. JK Woodward draws *Star Trek* comics and some of the *Doctor Who* comics. He and I celebrated our birthdays together. You do end up making these lifelong friendships.

I joined the Taylor Network of Podcasts. I believe being a part of a network is a tremendous asset because you always have other people who promote your stuff and vice versa. It's also helpful if you need an emergency guest or if you need to commiserate. It's nice to know you've got people who have your back.

I love getting feedback from my listeners, even when they're making fun of something I've said. One of my long-time sponsors makes these gothic perfumes with these crazy descriptions. I have to read the ad copy describing these weird perfumes at the start of every episode. People write to me all the time to ask, "does that actually smell good?" They'll make fun of some description I've given. I love it when people really listen and they come back at me with something that I said two years ago. I had somebody at a comic convention recognize me by my laugh. That makes you feel good. That's when you know people are really listening.

My advice to first-time podcasters is to invest in a good mic, and know that you're going to have some awkward episodes. Work your way through and just keep doing it. Keep honing it, keep pushing, keep getting your skills together.

Podcasting has changed my life. It's changed my whole network of friends, it's changed how I interact with people, and it's made me a better listener. I do hope to develop more relationships, where creators come to me when they have a new project that they want to promote. I want to have lifelong friendships with people, where they can always come back to my show and we can just keep building on our established camaraderie.

Wendi Freeman has appeared as host on *Double Page Spread* and *The Trashy Trio*

MARTHA W. SOUTHGATE is co-founder and brand manager of Southgate Media Group. She started SMG with her husband, Rob, as a creative outlet for their various interests and backgrounds. She also juggles homeschooling and parenting their 12-year-old daughter, Molly. Martha is an entrepreneur and passionately studies leadership and business development. She loves supporting and encouraging others by sharing her experiences and is about to release her first solo book and podcast, Broken to Brave.

ROBERT SOUTHGATE is co-founder and executive producer of Southgate Media Group (SMG). He has had various careers throughout his life, both in the creative world and the business sector. He was a professional actor in commercials and films, owned a high-end retail store, and is presently a content marketer with a focus on podcasting. Rob loves sharing ideas with others. He immerses himself in leadership and business development, has a strong passion for empowering others, and loves building into future leaders. Along with his wife, Martha, Rob started SMG as a creative outlet and a way to incorporate all of their interests and their past experiences. Rob is an entrepreneur with two Bachelors degrees in business (science of management and science of marketing) and an MBA in marketing from Roosevelt University. Most of all, Rob is the proud father of their daughter, Molly.

pliance

9 1 *